ENDORSEMENTS

Too frequently Christian teaching in our chu ~~~~~~~~~~~~~~~~~~
on imparting *correct doctrine* while neglecti ~~~~~~~~~~~~~~~~~
disciple's life necessary to achieve the true ~~~~~~~~~~~~~~~~~~
addressing the baptized as one situated in a particular cultural milieu and
(2) reorienting the disciple's personal *desires* now that they are "in Christ."
Masterfully, Dr. Espinosa offers a thoughtful and highly accessible distil-
lation of our holy faith that "sees through" our secular-consumer cultural
setting to the need of enlivening our passion for God, holiness, and truth.

Dr. Espinosa recognizes that dualities are at play in the Bible (e.g., flesh vs.
spirit, world vs. kingdom) and this duality comports well with Luther's articu-
lation of Christianity in terms of "contraries" or juxtapositions, even ironies.
He rightly argues that we are to live "under the contraries," not in Platonic
categories of *dualism* but a *duality* that is deeply spiritual *and* physical,
deeply ancient *and* current, deeply rooted in God's Law *and* Gospel, and
where the disciple persists as a sinner-saint—justified yet being sanctified—
in the face of the world's values and agenda.

The result is a fresh conversation about seeing *through* the eyes of faith
(a biblical sort of knowing, experiencing, and loving) that our identity is in
Christ Jesus and that God is in fact present how and where He said He
would be, and to clearly see all this in the midst of a culture that vies for our
very souls.

Rev. John J. Bombaro, PhD, LCDR, CHC, USNR
Grace Lutheran Church, San Diego, CA

Pastor Espinosa's new book, *Faith That Sees through the Culture*, is a
timely and important response to the moral relativism that has infected our
world today. There are constants and there are variables in life. God's Word
is the eternal truth that is the standard by which we must measure the status of our highly variable culture, not the other way around. This great book
plants the stake in the ground that God's Word, God's plan, and our faith are
the eternal truths. I highly commend his book.

Douglas S. Cavanaugh, Founder and CEO
The Ruby Restaurant Group

FAITH

THAT SEES THROUGH THE

CULTURE

ALFONSO ESPINOSA

CONCORDIA PUBLISHING HOUSE · SAINT LOUIS

Published by Concordia Publishing House
3558 S. Jefferson Avenue, St. Louis, MO 63118–3968
1-800-325-3040 • www.cph.org

Manufactured in the United States of America

Library of Congress Cataloging-in-Publication Data

Names: Espinosa, Alfonso O., author.
Title: Faith that sees through the culture : the Lutheran lens / by Alfonso
    O. Espinosa.
Description: St. Louis : Concordia Publishing House, 2018. | Includes
    bibliographical references and index.
Identifiers: LCCN 2017053977 (print) | LCCN 2018018660 (ebook) | ISBN
    9780758660107 | ISBN 9780758660046
Subjects: LCSH: Lutheran Church--Doctrines. | Christianity and culture.
Classification: LCC BX8065.3 (ebook) | LCC BX8065.3 .E83 2018 (print) | DDC
    230/.41--dc23
LC record available at https://lccn.loc.gov/2017053977

1 2 3 4 5 6 7 8 9 10   27 26 25 24 23 22 21 20 19 18

DEDICATION TO TRACI DAWN ESPINOSA:

"When I look at all the women in the world, I find none of whom I could boast as I boast with joyful conscience of my own." —Martin Luther

AND TO OUR CHILDREN, A. J., Elizabeth, Danielle, Christina, David James, Esbeydi, Bryan, and Katherine:

"Behold, children are a heritage from the LORD." —Psalm 127:3

ACKNOWLEDGMENTS

I wish to thank my congregation—St. Paul's Lutheran Church of Irvine (formerly of Laguna Beach)—for granting me a seventh-year sabbatical. Without them, this work would have remained an idea. I thank them for their love and support.

I ran my proposal by my father confessor, Rev. Robert Dargatz. He was wise to remind me that when it comes to the theological dualities, we must take special care. If one goes too far to one side, we end up with heresy. We must be faithful to both ends of the theological spectrum. I'm reminded that pastors are fortunate to have their own pastors. Another pastor with whom I work on the LCMS Board for National Mission is Rev. Tim Droegemueller. He and I conducted a little word study in St. Louis and discovered how the Scriptures describe the Christian with despair and without it, depending on the context. This motivated me all the more to write a book to those Christians feeling despair, so that in faith they would also have joy and be delivered from despair.

During the sabbatical, I had some quality time in Germany visiting my daughter Danielle and our new grandson, as well as our son-in-law Simon Volkmar, who is serving as a vicar at a SELK congregation in Düsseldorf. I had the chance to bounce some ideas off my theologically minded son-in-law. He was a good listener, and I'm grateful for his help in empathizing with modern readers who are serious about their faith but are also carrying around good questions. My wife, Traci, and I traveled with our eldest daughter, Elizabeth. I ran many of the real-life anecdotes by her and she offered quality suggestions, true to her professional counselor training.

I share many stories from a ministry spanning almost three decades, and I have learned how the Holy Spirit also teaches through the parishioners I have been called to serve. They have the Word of Christ dwelling in them and they have blessed me. Most of the stories within this book are about them (with some exceptions). I have changed the names and other personal details so as to protect identities. In those cases where I've retained their actual name with a few other true details, I gathered their permission to do so. Of course, many other parishioners not mentioned in the book's anecdotes have also helped me tremendously.

One of those former members I served is Mrs. Joni Breland. I mention her because she has been among those Christians who have taught me that we can know all the good theology in the world, but if we can't meaningfully communicate it to real people, what good is it? I've written this while trying to take deep truths of God's Holy Word and then present them in ways that can be grasped without a degree in theology. I hope I've come close to accomplishing this.

I have felt invigorated by how the team at Concordia Publishing House has received my proposals for this book. Paul McCain, Scot Kinnaman, and Laura Lane gave me the confidence needed to finish. The LCMS is blessed to have such an outstanding and faithful publishing house.

Finally, I thank my wife, Traci. She has helped me in countless ways to be the kind of preacher, teacher, and writer that I am. I asked her to listen to a lot of material. She always had good feedback. She is true to life and seeks the practical so that our sacred teaching doesn't fly too high above our heads. Her encouragement to me is priceless, and she reminds me that we can do all things through Christ who strengthens us (Philippians 4:13).

TABLE OF CONTENTS

Acknowledgments 6

Foreword 10

Preface 14

Introduction 16

Chapter 1: Struggling with the Outside 22

Chapter 2: Struggling on the Inside 34

Chapter 3: Reality Check—Christian 44

Chapter 4: Reality Check—Disciple 63

Chapter 5: Reality Check—Priest 75

Chapter 6: The Lutheran Lens—What Is Real? 89

Chapter 7: The Lutheran Lens—What Am I? 111

Chapter 8: The Lutheran Lens—
To Whom Am I Speaking? 128

Chapter 9: The Lutheran Lens—Where Are We? 160

Chapter 10: The Lutheran Lens—When Are We? 189

Chapter 11: The Lutheran Lens—What Do I Say? 209

Chapter 12: The Lutheran Lens—Convergence,
20/20 Vision 241

Bibliography 256

Topical Index 258

Scripture Index 261

FOREWORD

SIMPLE COMPLEXITIES

The teaching of God's Word can never be distilled down to platitudes. Instead, God's Word confronts the believer with irreducible tensions such as Law and Gospel, the two natures in Christ, the death of God's eternal Son on the cross, and so forth. Not only are these bipolarities common in the structure of the Christian faith, but they all maintain interpenetrating tensions among themselves. What I mean is that what we believe about the person of Christ is related to what we think happened to our Lord on the cross, and that that relationship between who Christ is and what He does on the cross is also intimately tied to the Church's proclamation in Law and Gospel. Without too much effort, we are tying together a number of ways of "looking at" the Christian religion and her teaching. This intense complexity of our teaching takes into account both the actual instruction of God from Holy Scripture and how that teaching from Scripture impacts the messy daily lives of Christians, actual human beings within culture. Once applied, this Word of God intersects with the Christian faith as it is lived in the lives of those who are simultaneously righteous and sinners. One can immediately see why soul care requires thoughtful and theologically trained pastors. One of those is the author of this present volume, a dear colleague, Al Espinosa. He helps us deal with this complexity simply. Both pastor and layman will be helped by this work.

Dealing with this complexity is one of the great challenges of Christianity in the modern world, partly because irony is not the strong suit of the modern intellectual context. We moderns demand that things be explained in a straightforward, uncomplicated way. Intellectual indirection today is criticized as cant, wordy dogma, or out-and-out contradiction. At best, irony is a word game, not a hint to the interwoven and complex character of reality in the presence of a gracious God. Irony is thought to be fun and entertaining but cannot be a description of what is. When my family talks about the horror movies my older daughter likes to watch, my wife is revolted by the content, and my daughter replies, "But it's not real." In the same way, we tolerate ambiguities in movies only because "it isn't real." I love reading the great literary novels because they often subtly confront the reader with the kinds of challenges that give rise to the indirection that deep consideration of life and reality are made of. It isn't that reality's character is unclear— just more complex than we can make out at first glance. The same can be said about our Christian religion, especially as it makes an impact in the morally untidy world in which we live.

God is always "turning over" things on us, making a mockery of our expectations. For example, all too easily we think that the best and brightest have a right to the Kingdom; it is theirs by reason of their talent, ability, and shining good works. Nothing could be more wrong, for those who are beloved by God are loved for Christ's sake, not because of their own attainments. And though they appear rejected by God and outcasts from the world, they are the exact opposite (Matthew 5:1–12). They are treasures of God purchased by the cleansing blood of Christ and sons of God by adoption into God's family through the word of God's Son.

How easily our heart gets us down, though, when confronted by our own weakness and the tribulations that we face daily. Sometimes I wonder, "What's wrong with me?" Perhaps you have felt the same way. It points out to me that things can't be as perfect as I want them to be or try to make them.

Here we need to retreat from our experience to the Word of God to seek comfort under what Martin Luther calls *contraria*: "the contraries." God exercises our faith by setting before us our own weakness and telling us that the weak are blessed. We feel no such thing in our hearts! So where are we left? Not depending on our hearts, but depending entirely upon the Word of God. He promises that those who do not have a deed will inherit the promised land, like our forefather in the faith, Abraham. He promises that those who do not bear children will be mothers of uncounted myriads, like Sarah (Galatians 4). So when we see that we have not and do not, then we should confess that we are truly blessed, purely because the Word says so. What we have is Christ. He has done everything.

All of the Christian life is then lived *sub contraria*, that is, "under the contraries." Luther taught that God is always hiding His grace and blessings under the signs of those things that our human reason declines to believe to be capable of bearing the blessings of God. To exercise our faith, our heavenly Father plans that our strength should be made perfect in weakness (2 Corinthians 12:9), that our faith is set in its substance without seeing (Hebrews 11:1), that winning is losing (Philippians 3:7–8), that only sinners are forgiven (Psalm 32:1–2), and that life is gained only by death (2 Corinthians 4:10–11). You don't get much more contrary than that.

Our ignorance about the contraries relates to the fallen nature of humanity. We don't see clearly because of our spiritual blindness. In that blindness, we begin to impose a shape and meaning on reality that is foreign to its complexity and contrariety. In no area of human life is this more significant than in the experience of human suffering and weakness. For example, life is not just so simple as to be described as the effort to avoid suffering or to seek the greatest pleasure, as Thomas Hobbes argued. Such simplistic interpretations of reality founder on the pervasive and indivisible complexity of things in our experience. Experiences we might call "bittersweet" are examples of the lack of simplicity in real life.

Motivational speakers say, "What does not kill you will make your stronger." This is not the whole story for Christians. For those shaped under the cross of Christ, what does kill us does make us stronger, and that strength is hidden under weakness in the cross that God sends. At its very core, Christianity has this complexity, the complexity of the cross, returning us to the completeness with which we were created in Eden. The cross, its suffering and death both hide and confer life, peace, and joy. Our own suffering and anxiety over the human condition must never keep us from seeing that God Himself triumphs in us through such things, all hidden under the contraries. This is the "seeing through" of which this book speaks. And it's just that simple.

Scott R. Murray, PhD
The Commemoration of the Cappadocian Fathers, 2018

PREFACE

I feel like the luckiest guy in the world to get to do what I get to do. I'm referring to the pastor-teacher ministry (Ephesians 4) and the call to share and equip people with the Word of the Lord Jesus Christ. And yet, I've always been what I see as a middle-zone guy. That is, the Lord has equipped me in His sacred teaching as a PhD in theology; an adjunct professor of theology at Concordia University, Irvine; a writer with contributions to *The Lutheran Study Bible* and *The Lutheran Difference*; and a pastor for over twenty-six years. Yet there are teachers finer than I, and at the highest levels of the Church's teaching ministry (and indeed even in the parish ministry). My position, therefore, is that of a servant in the middle, so my passion has been to reach God's people with the best of God's teaching in a way that is meaningful and easy to understand. I strive to be a bridge for bringing the most important teachings of God's Word to the everyday Christian who often struggles like every other Christian out there (including myself).

That general vision has been narrowed recently to a specific concern about the area of the "both-and" dualities in the Word of Christ. There are so many "two sides of the same coin" in the Word of truth. For example, we correctly confess that God works upon us so that (1) God kills us, and (2) God makes us alive. He uses His Word to do the one and He uses His Word to do the other. In doing so, however, He reveals that the Word itself is a "both-and" Word, a two-sided Word, a two-themed Word. It is duality. It is used one way in one context and another way in another context. And this is just one example of the many dualities that exist in the Christian faith.

When people are not aware of these dualities, however, then they begin to assume that either only one side is true and the other side must be false, or they give in to the skepticism of our time and culture, and they begin to suspect that

God's Word is contradictory. Often, many folks won't necessarily ever get to the point of openly criticizing the Word of God, but in their heart and mind, they begin to feel that God's Word is just beyond them—not accessible as perhaps they had hoped it would be or could be. This is a sad state of affairs. I am motivated not to stand for this. I was inspired to do something about this problem. This is the theological reason that this book exists.

The book also exists, however, for practical reasons. I was blessed that for the first time in my service as a pastor, my congregation at St. Paul's Lutheran Church of Irvine, California, chose to grant me a sabbatical. They also permitted me to put most of my vacation time alongside the one-month sabbatical so that I could be away for two solid months. Knowing that this was coming up, I reached out to the team at Concordia Publishing House and was invited to float a proposal for a book that would serve serious and mature Christians who recognize the challenges of living the faith in the twenty-first century. I thought about this for a solid month, and that was when my concern about the lack of awareness of Christian dualities came to the surface.

How can Christians live more confidently in their faith if they are at the same time constantly challenged to understand it? The dualities can be confusing. Something should be done about it, so I submitted my proposal to CPH. I was delighted by the response. They agreed to my proposal, and the Lord gave me two months to write this book. It is written by me—the middle-zone guy—attempting to write about some of the most challenging teachings of the saving faith in a way that can be easily grasped. I pray that it is a blessing to you, the reader.

INTRODUCTION

This book is entitled *Faith That Sees through the Culture.* That's a long title, but what does this mean? That's the Lutheran question. The first word, *faith*, is a created thing, and this one point by itself already represents why this book is speaking differently than much of popular Christianity in America. In today's parlance, *faith* is an exertion of will; it is a decision. Perhaps some would say it is a decision enabled by a *prevenient* grace, a kind of preliminary or empowering grace, but nonetheless the key player is the person who uses his or her volition to believe: God has done His part; now our part is faith. This is *not* the definition this book is working with.

Faith, while it eventually impacts every faculty of a person—*including* the will (so that faith is experienced also in the will)—is not reduced to an action of the will. It is a gift from God that God must bring into existence. This is why the old Lutheran teachers described faith as a *spiritual organ*. Just as God created one's heart and lungs, God created one's faith. As the heart pumps blood, faith pumps prayer, service, and witness. For this to happen, however, the Word of Jesus must be received. Romans 10:17 teaches that "faith comes . . . through the word of Christ." Through the Word of Christ, God creates and preserves. If this faith is to survive and grow, therefore, it must receive the Word of Christ over and over again.

This faith comes therefore with a significant presupposition: the Christian with such faith is always around the Word of Christ, and if this is the case, then such a Christian is always around His Sacraments too (since His Word prescribes His Sacraments). These gifts of Word and Sacraments sustain and nourish faith, keeping it alive. This faith is therefore also *sacramental*.

Many years ago, during my undergrad years, a classmate in my doctrine class was frustrated by the several ways the Word of Christ comes to people. He asked my old professor, who was a particularly gifted man, "But why the redundancy? Why is it necessary that the Word come in so many varying ways?" I could feel the background skepticism: the presentation sounded like religion for the sake of religion; people had just made up additional ways to receive God's grace. The only problem with this pessimistic suspicion is that God's Word teaches about the various means of the Word of Christ. These are not man's idea but God's. Why on earth would God do this?

I've had a lot of time to think about my old classmate's concern and I have come to appreciate the analogy of holy marriage. In marriage, husband and wife are called by God to love each other, but suppose a spouse tried to reduce that love to a singular expression. Imagine a husband telling his wife, "You know that I love you since I wear my wedding band." What if the husband said this with the belief that he was therefore exempt from every other expression of love? That is, this husband believed that serving his wife, encouraging her with his words, caressing her with his touch, and giving her intimate attention was completely unnecessary. "Why do these things, when my love is already affirmed by the ring I wear?" How might the wife react? These considerations remind us that marital love is supposed to be expressed in *many* ways. This is God's design, and God knows what He is doing. We should trust Him.

This is also true when it comes to receiving the Word of Christ. God has intentionally given many ways of receiving Jesus' Word, because God knows how much help we need. He knows how easy it is for us to grow discouraged. He understands our great need to be strengthened in many ways and on many fronts. God knows what He is doing. We should trust Him.

In saying this we have presented a duality that this book takes for granted. God gives His Word not only to be preached (and heard and believed), but also to be encountered physically, on our bodies in Holy Baptism, and into our bodies in Holy Communion. Water is to be poured out upon the Christian (and this water contains the Word); bread and wine are to be taken into the mouth (and these also give the body and blood of Jesus Christ). No one can explain how these things are possible. It is enough that God says they happen. Faith believes in what God says. Interestingly, these take hold of the person to give faith, and then, when faith is created, faith takes hold of what God's Word has already done. Talk about a complementary relationship. In this way, important questions are answered: "Shouldn't a person have faith when they are baptized?" Answer: "Yes." "But you say that Baptism is most often given to those—especially infants—without faith." Answer: "True." "Well then, I'm confused." Answer: "Baptism creates the faith required to receive it."

See the duality: Jesus comes through what is written and what is poured out; Jesus comes through what is taught and through what is eaten. God's plan is Word *and* Sacraments. Not just one, but both. Interestingly, the Christian faith has held on to this duality for two thousand years, even while many contemporary Christians have sadly given up on the Sacraments, convinced that they seem too much like religion for the sake of religion. We should never, however, give up on God's gifts just because it is possible for some to mishandle them. This book holds to the old tradition taught in God's Word. It does so because this book assumes that God's Word is powerful and effects the miraculous, not to tickle the fancy of people through the visually spectacular, but to grant them God's grace for eternal life. The Sacraments are therefore anything but religion for the sake of religion.

What this book does, however, is look at some monumentally important dualities that are especially lost on today's culture. There is not enough space to include all important dualities. There are many that this book does not elaborate upon. The duality above all others is that the Savior, Jesus Christ, is true God and true man. This important duality of Christ will have to be studied elsewhere. Other dualities not presented are more basic, like life and death, light and darkness, angels and demons, and the way of the wise versus the way of the fool (though what is covered here is related even to these dualities). There are many more. The good news, however, is that this book is discussing some great ones and—again—ones that need more attention in the face of the cultural challenges that Christians face today.

To speak of the ability *to see* and to *be seeing* through faith echoes what St. Paul talks about in 2 Corinthians 5:7: "For we walk by faith, not by sight." The *seeing* in our title therefore is not a physical seeing, but a *faith* seeing. Faith *sees* what is otherwise unseen; faith *knows* what otherwise is unknown. This is what created faith does. It is the ability to perceive the things of God that the rest of the world considers to be nonsense.

Such seeing is needed on account of where we live: in the culture. The title of the book does not assume that the culture in itself is bad. As we will explain, the culture includes many things in God's good creation (and yes, the creation continues to be good). At the same time, the culture also includes many things that are not so good. These are the things we are bringing out, not so we can sit on a high horse to condemn the culture, but to know how to respond to the culture through faith. Along the way, this book recommends that the culture should be considered something holy. This will be explained even in the face of its many contours to the contrary. In the meantime, the culture includes everything that fills our everyday lives in our day-to-day existence and where we live. It includes what we eat, what we listen to, how we live together; how we work and how we play; and how we dress and how we communicate. Culture is pervasive. Along the way, it is for the Christian to know how to live in it.

Finally, the dualities—or lenses—are biblical, and because they are biblical, they are also *Lutheran*. As many know, the Lutheran Church in its original form called itself *evangelical*; that is, "of the evangel," or "of the Gospel." It is a Christian *confession* that emphasizes a Christ-centered approach to the Christian faith. That makes sense since even the word *Christian* means "Christ's" or "belonging to Christ." In this way, the Lutheran Christian maintains that a Christ-centered emphasis is really the only proper emphasis. Many have summarized the Lutheran approach in terms of the great *solas* of the Reformation: grace alone, faith alone, Scripture alone, and in Christ alone. For our lens to be *Lutheran*, it must emphasize the saving Gospel of Jesus Christ more than anything else. Just one more qualification here: over the years, many denominations (which is more of a sociological label than a theological one) have forsaken the confession that the Holy Bible is the inspired and inerrant Word of God. Sadly, some Lutheran traditions have also turned away from inspiration and inerrancy. This book, however, has held on to the old confession and continues the tradition that the Holy Bible is God's true Word.

With this foundation, we go forward on this journey of *Faith That Sees through the Culture*. Chapters 1 and 2 empathize with all true Christians who know the external and internal struggles that come with life. These do not mean the Christian is not a true Christian. Much to the contrary, all Christians endure these assaults. This is the norm, not the exception. Chapters 3, 4, and 5 fortify the Christian's true identity in the midst of the struggles, thus providing confidence and security. The believer in Christ is *Christian* (chapter 3), *disciple* (chapter 4), and *priest* (chapter 5). With the believer's identity firmly established, the book launches into the most important lenses, or dualities, presented in this volume. Those lenses are the following: the duality of the visible and invisible (chapter 6); the duality of the old and new aspects of the Christian (chapter 7); the duality of approaching others with a Gospel that is both inclusive and exclusive (chapter 8); the duality of church and state (chapter 9); the duality of living both in the present and in the future (chapter 10); and the duality of the two ways of speaking God's Word: the duality of Law and Gospel (chapter 11). Chapter 12 is a summary of all these and how to pull them out, depending on what the culture throws at the Christian. It is time to start our journey. This is faith that sees through the culture.

CHAPTER 1

STRUGGLING
WITH
THE
OUTSIDE

Culture consists of everything that fills the lives of people in a given place, be it the clothing they wear, the food they eat, the music they listen to, or the way in which their communities are organized. These things are connected to the good work of God in creation, but also in some cases to the effects of sin in the world, which contribute to cultural formation. This reminds us that while the culture and God's creation we live in are related, they are not the same thing. While it may be necessary therefore to discern what is bad in the culture, we should never say—just because sin has entered the creation—that God's creation is bad. It isn't, and who can deny its marvelous benefits?

THE GOOD CREATION

In the beginning, God beheld a "very good" creation (Genesis 1:31), and even now—in spite of sin—the creation is still just that. Look upon a gorgeous sunset or take in a splendid moonlit night. These punctuate the "very good." We rejoice to confess, "The heavens declare the glory of God, and the sky above proclaims His handiwork" (Psalm 19:1). This is always true. Thank God.

Many of creation's "very good things" slide into the cultures formed by people. We praise God for art that inspires, celebrations of joy marked by delicious food and calming drink, and sports that make us jump up and down as we cheer. Just look at a pug tilting its head, and try not to smile; or a pouncing kitten, and try not to laugh. See a dolphin launch from ocean depths not far from the edge of your boat, or witness the aurora borealis for the first time, without letting the moment take over. Witness a healthy baby born, and try not to be in awe. In the Apostles' Creed, when we confess God as Creator, we acknowledge Him as the giver of all good gifts. We acknowledge Him in the explanation of the First Article that He is the Giver of house and home and all that comes with these. Solomon was expressing wisdom when he wrote, "Go, eat your bread with joy, and drink your wine with a merry heart, for God has already approved what you do" (Ecclesiastes 9:7). God approves of our enjoyment of the good things in His creation!

God's very good creation and the idea of the world, however, take us back to the distinction between culture and creation mentioned above. This can be a little confusing because the word *world* has more than one meaning. If *world* is used for "earth," then we are back to the realm of the very good creation; but *world* may also stand for the existence we inhabit, and that includes the evil influences in the sphere of our lives: bad things in the culture with bad spiritual influences behind them.

"THE WORLD" AS DISTINCT FROM CREATION

There is therefore a bad world within God's very good creation. The saying goes, "Christians are *in* the world, but not *of* the world." This sounds compelling (at least catchy), but is it true? The sinful world seems inescapable. Evil influences permeate the culture, and we are very much in the culture. *World* in the sense of sinful *worldliness* is in the air we breathe. We go to the cinema to watch a movie that we thought we wanted to see, but it ends up being offensive and degrading. Welcome to the world.

This world comes with what feels like an irresistible pull, an unholy tractor beam. The physical earth exerts gravity that firmly plants us on terra firma, but there's something else—something spiritual—that pulls us down. The tug of the world splashes spiritual mud and grime on our consciences. It makes us feel dirty.

We can't get away from it either. Even if we tried, the best we could do is leave one mud pit for another. We're stuck and it makes it seem as though our faith is stuck too. When darkness envelopes, faith can feel ineffectual, insignificant, and irrelevant. The light of faith seems to grow dim when surrounded by thick clouds shutting out faith.

The world impacted by sin means we encounter outbursts of anger, violence, destruction, and deception from others against us; physical illness, since sin leads to death; all turmoil, strife, and division, skepticism and unbelief, sensuality and lust; the pursuit of power and greed, which can easily disrupt our jobs and security; and manipulative forces that treat people as being dispensable. The world can hurt us. It tries to.

That is to say the evil forces in the world do not simply put a negative pall over the environment—as if worldly evil simply made life gloomier—but this spiritual condition within the culture can bring forces pinpointed against us. The Christian can be persecuted by the world. The Lord Jesus acknowledged as much in the Sermon on the Mount. The Lord taught, as recorded in Matthew 5:10, "Blessed are those who are persecuted for righteousness' sake, for theirs is the kingdom of heaven." The promise of the kingdom of heaven is encouraging and sweet, but the persecution on account of a life lived according to God's righteousness? Not so inspirational. We don't get all warm and fuzzy inside at the promise of persecution. The world, however, shouts at the Christian, "Be more tolerant," even when the Christian's faith is no longer tolerated. This is a catch-22, but the world doesn't care. All it wants is for Christians to shut up already and keep their religion to themselves.

And as if this state of affairs isn't bad enough, it gets worse.

THE DEVIL

The world is only half of what stands against us from the outside. God's Word also warns, "Be sober-minded; be watchful. Your adversary the devil prowls around like a roaring lion, seeking someone to devour" (1 Peter 5:8). The world is not the only external cause of sin; so are the devil and demons. This is where we start to lose people. It is one thing to acknowledge social maladies and to possibly permit that there is something abstract called "evil" out there in the culture, but a personal being called "the devil"? This is hard for some folks to accept.

The New Testament, however, won't permit us to argue that the Scriptures present a worldview that does not differentiate between physical and spiritual maladies. The New Testament is full of medical diagnoses of physical ailments. Leprosy, hemorrhaging, and fevers are not said to be from the demonic. Distinct from these physical ailments, however, are certain spiritual conditions in Scripture that require exorcism. These conditions are clearly attributed to the demonic. Even apart from possession, the apostle Paul himself suffered the effects of "a thorn . . . in the flesh, a messenger of Satan" (2 Corinthians 12:7). We don't know how this manifested itself, but we do know that it caused the apostle to suffer.

These spiritual assaults from the evil one remind us that he was a murderer from the beginning (see John 8:44). His mission is to destroy and to lead others to join his condemned state. He is the ultimate reminder that misery loves company. Again, he wants to devour (see 1 Peter 5:8), and he fires flaming darts/missiles at God's children (see Ephesians 6:16). All of this means that we can feel as though we are under spiritual attack.

EVEN CHRISTIANS CAN DESPAIR

Marilyn had phoned to set up an appointment for pastoral counsel. I knew just from the brief time on the phone that she was very upset. I had no idea how serious it was. She was a lifelong Christian and had held the Lutheran Confession for many years. She was an active member and in good standing in my congregation. She seemed to be a healthy Christian.

When she arrived at my study, her brokenness was visceral. I was already aware of her failed marriage, but it felt as though all the pain of that divorce had come back, and it came back at a terrible time because Marilyn had just been informed that her company was letting her go. She was now unemployed, and this while trying to provide for her young child and her brother who had recently sustained a brain injury. She was lonely, she was angry, and she was terrified. She was a mess. And she felt the weight of these things piling upon her like huge, crushing boulders. In the midst of the pressure, she was now having a crisis of faith. She knew that God's mercy is a gift, nothing she had to earn, but where was He when she needed Him most?

What made this moment in time so difficult was not just what she said but the way she said it. She was in agony. I felt as though I was witnessing someone falling into an abyss of despair. In other words, it was more than the real hardships confronting her from the world of broken promises and perhaps some unsavory politics at the job; these things were combined with a spiritual element. Marilyn felt as though she was losing her faith.

This is the external assault against all Christians, and we need help for faith to see through such circumstances. We need help when we feel especially powerless. We need help to walk by faith and not by sight, because what we see is often distressing. There are times when the Christian might feel despair. St. Paul described his own experience with his fellow missionaries: "We were so utterly burdened beyond our strength that we despaired of life itself" (2 Corinthians 1:8). If you have ever felt this way, you're not alone.

EVIL IN THE BROADER CULTURE

But what happens when the stain of sin and the attacks of the evil one come upon whole societies? What happens when the disease reaches national proportions?

In the history of the world, great civilizations were just that, once upon a time—great. Until they collapsed upon themselves. No longer great, but destroyed. Why? It seems a gross oversimplification, but there is truth involved: they became so in love with created things that they lost track of the Creator.

The Northern Kingdom of Israel is a case study. The political and social conditions as they approached the Assyrian catastrophe in 722 BC were ripe for implosion. The collapse came after crass immorality had taken over. Israel became too worldly for her own good. In the days of the prophet Amos, Israel had regained her former splendor as in the days of Solomon. A time of prosperity was upon the nation, but it was a prosperity that could not hide what was corrupt and rotten underneath.

Part of the problem was that life became too easy. For example, Israel leading up to 722 BC did not know enemy oppression. It had not known warfare. How might these conditions apply to American generations? There is the so-called greatest generation. Consider their time: They grew up during the Great Depression and they experienced World War II. Hardship brought the need to fight, not only against real political enemies but against laziness and living for self. Israel got to a generation that wasn't fighting anymore but grew fat on self-indulgence.

Business and commerce were back to the levels of the glory days of the united kingdom under David and Solomon. Building flourished and the nation was proud. A haughty spirit was the status quo. Luxuries were insisted upon and homes became palaces. The rich were no longer satisfied with only one home. It got to a ridiculous point. We learn from 1 Kings 22:39 that Ahab built an ivory house. This wasn't reserved for the king, though; Amos describes the nation in terms of "houses of ivory" (Amos 3:15).

But alongside the super-rich homes was also extreme poverty. It had reached the point that some of the people were sold into slavery. There was deceit and oppression. There was no pity for the poor, and violence and robbery were commonplace. This, however, was just the half of it.

The immorality had a spiritual component. The nation lost the hallmark of her theocratic identity: the worship of the Lord and only the Lord. She entered idolatry, the worship of false gods. Jeroboam I made idolatry the official religion of the Northern Kingdom. With idolatry came other problems, like superstition and witchcraft. The occult flourished. Enough was enough. God let Assyria completely take over Israel.

Someone might object to comparing the United States to a theocratic nation. The United States is not that. We're a republic, and many identify with an extreme version of the separation of church and state. This distinction, however, cannot escape the basic problem. If one insists that our case study not be a theocratic nation like Israel, then so be it. If we search for a nation in history more similar to our polytheistic and secular state, then consider Rome. Rome became so corrupt that she could no longer sustain herself. Worldliness can destroy any nation.

It would be a mistake, however, to reduce the corrosion of a nation to a lack of morality. There is always a spiritual condition—and practice—in the backdrop. Indeed, the United States of America, though being "secular," is not a nation without spirituality. Secularism is not synonymous with atheism. Most citizens claim some sort of belief system. Luther wrote in the Large Catechism, "You can easily see and sense how the world practices only false worship and idolatry. For no people have ever been so corrupt that they did not begin and continue some divine worship. Everyone has set up as his special god whatever he looked to for blessings, help, and comfort."[1] This is still happening. And where the world does its best to deny the one true God, the evil one is also there, keeping us religious, but in the wrong ways.

We are, however, reminded: "Just let not the devil and the world deceive you with their show, which indeed remains for a time, but finally is nothing."[2]

TWO-PRONGED ATTACK FROM THE OUTSIDE

This external one-two punch, therefore, confronts us both individually and corporately. And when it happens, it is easy for even lifelong Christians to enter a faith crisis. We're living in this mess and it's not difficult to find Christians bewildered

---

1   LC I 17.
2   LC I 46.

as to how to live out their faith in a world so dead set against it. How do we even begin to shine the light of faith under such conditions?

There are many reasons to wonder. A colleague in the ministry once shared that he had been given the opportunity to thoroughly communicate the saving Gospel to a close friend. His presentation was buttressed by solid apologetics demonstrating the reliability of the biblical text as well as evidence for the resurrection of Jesus Christ. His witness to the sin problem condemning us to death was powerful; and his testimony to the pure saving Gospel leading to life and salvation was pristine. The Spirit of God was with my fellow pastor. His friend listened carefully. At the end of the time for consideration for what God has done for us in His Son, Jesus Christ, for our justification and reconciliation (Romans 5), the friend was finally ready to respond: "I am convinced that everything you've shared with me is true." This was cause for elation, but then the friend continued, "But I can't accept it right now, because I'm having too much fun." He was quite simply unwilling to give up his entanglements with the world and his compact with the devil.

How can faith see through this cultural, worldly, and demonic situation? Again, we need help, but first we must continue to understand the full extent of our predicament. When we do understand, when the lens of our faith becomes clearer, then we are no longer mastered by the world and the enemy.

Remember Marilyn? At the end of the day, there was only one thing I could offer her. Through the Word of Christ, Holy Absolution, and the intentional return to her Holy Baptism into Jesus Christ (all of this was a return to the Word), I witnessed—over time—a transformation. Where hopelessness once reigned, faith rose up, and I saw my sister in Christ become stronger than she had ever been. Still, it is vital for us to have a full view of what we are up against. It's not just the stuff that confronts us from the outside but also that which causes us to be embattled from within.

STRUGGLING WITH THE OUTSIDE

UNCOVER INFORMATION

1. How does one differentiate between the concept of *culture* and the concept of *creation*?

2. Explain the two ways in which the word *world* is used.

3. How does Scripture describe the *devil*?

4. How can whole nations show signs of evil?

5. Describe *despair*.

DISCOVER MEANING

1. What about the culture should we thank God for and embrace? What about the culture should we guard against?

2. How does 1 John 2:15–17 describe the *world*?

3. Besides the fact that it seems contrary to Scripture, what's wrong with reducing the devil to an abstraction?

4. In considering the overall nation, what is the seeming association between crass immorality and what is believed in? How can these undermine a nation?

5. Can a Christian with genuine faith go through despair? Why or why not?

EXPLORE IMPLICATIONS

1. Consider this statement: Christians are in the world, but not of the world. Do you agree? Why or why not?

2. If you agree with the above statement, how does the Christian live in the balance?

3. How might the devil's attempts to "devour" and the unleashing of his flaming darts/missiles translate into what we experience in life?

4. Luther's quote about the world setting up false worship and idolatry is an important warning. How do these impact the Christian seeking to live in true faith?

5. If a Christian is in despair, what might help him or her?

CHAPTER 2

STRUGGLING
ON
THE
INSIDE

I hit the jackpot when the Lord led me to my wife, Traci. She is an amazing woman. My life is a hundred times better because of her. What fills me with joy is remembering what we've been through together and what she has said and done along the way. She once told me, "I love you so much that I would live in a cardboard box with you." One summer, she almost did.

THE GIFT OF CONTENTMENT

We were in a summer vicarage parsonage in the inner city. We were poor. There was hardly any furniture in that old house. In our little living room, we had this interesting red velvet love seat. A folding chair served as a stand for our nine-inch television, which was good for five or six channels. In those days if we scrounged up enough change to go out and get ice-cream cones, we were happy as larks. That summer, my wife proved to me that her words were true. She really would live anywhere with me.

One night a homeless man came to our door, asking for food. My wife went to work and for a moment, I thought she was the widow of Zarephath for whom Elijah worked a mighty miracle, as she was given a jar of flour and jug of oil that wouldn't run out (1 Kings 17). For the most part I was convinced that we didn't have much of anything to offer, but my wife cooked up an amazing plate full of piping-hot and scrumptious food. Where did this food come from? I was genuinely surprised by what she produced from our humble kitchen, and the homeless man ate like a king that evening.

Our experience, though, pales in comparison with what my mother knew growing up during the Great Depression. When she was little, she and her several siblings lived with my grandparents in a village-like community. Her family had two separate cabins/rooms. One cabin was a bedroom for the whole family. It had a wooden floor and a wood-burning heater with a chimney. Most of the floor in the other cabin was also wood, except where a wood-burning stove sat on the dirt. This cabin had a table, and everyone sat on wooden boxes for chairs. The bathrooms were community outhouses, and everyone in the village shared water faucets. There was no electricity, and at night, kerosene lamps provided what was needed to see. Washboards were used for cleaning clothes, and one made the most of the breeze, hanging clothes on clotheslines to dry. Beans, rice, and eggs were staples; tortillas, a standard delight.

And my mother said she was happy growing up. She also said, "You don't miss what you never had." My dad had similar stories, including the fact that for at least one Christmas, the family Christmas tree was a tumbleweed. As a kid, he also played kick the can. He said it was fun. That's all they had, and they were happy.

St. Paul wrote to St. Timothy, "Godliness with contentment is great gain, for we brought nothing into the world, and we cannot take anything out of the world" (1 Timothy 6:6–7). And yet even with the possibility of helping ourselves against the external problems from the world and the evil one, we are not content with simplicity. We have an insatiable appetite for more, and if we are not careful, we can hurt ourselves.

DRAWN TO THE WORLD

My wife and I no longer live in that inner-city parsonage. Our house is bigger and we have a lot more stuff. The televisions (plural) far surpass nine inches; we get more than half a dozen channels; we eat better than we did; and our furniture is a considerable improvement. I am convinced, however, that none of this really makes us happier than we were. In fact, I often miss those days. They were less complicated. There were fewer distractions, and what was most important in life was magnified: our faith, our family, and our love.

Unfortunately, it feels like a tractor beam for wanting more is always activated, and we tend to align ourselves with it. We steer our own ship so as to synchronize with what is often a sinful allurement. This is where we contribute to the madness. This is where we shoot ourselves in the foot. And some would say that this propensity within us is getting worse. The Lutheran Confessions state flatly, "Man's nature is gradually growing weaker as the world grows older."[3]

It is one thing that the world threatens us as it does, but it is another thing for us to be so friendly toward it. "Do not love the world or the things in the world. If anyone loves the world, the love of the Father is not in him. For all that is in the world—the desires of the flesh and the desires of the eyes and pride of life [that is, pride in possessions]—is not from the Father but is from the world" (1 John 2:15–16). We feel convicted the moment we read or hear this holy passage. We know it's true precisely because we know that our desires and pride are worldly and not of the Father.

3   AC XXIII 14.

God's Word warns us about these things: "Beloved, I urge you as sojourners and exiles to abstain from the passions of the flesh, which wage war against your soul" (1 Peter 2:11). This internal struggle is serious business. The evil is not just in the culture; it is in us, and it is capable of destroying us.

How did this happen? We are connected to our first parents, whose rebellion represented what any of us in their position would have done. That rebellion cost us all, because what we call in the Church *original sin* is inherited sin. Their curse is now our curse; "And in sin did [our] mother[s] conceive [us]" (Psalm 51:5). We are not sinful because of sinful things we've done; we do sinful things because we are sinful.

God's holy command was given: "But of the tree of the knowledge of good and evil you shall not eat, for in the day that you eat of it you shall surely die" (Genesis 2:17). They were duly warned. When they were without sin, this command was no burden, but a delight to keep. They had Paradise, and following God's command was a way of celebrating their being in His image and likeness. The command was no dangling carrot; rather, it was a sign of freedom.

THE LOSS OF THE IMAGE OF GOD

In spite of all this, they rebelled—and they died from within. The image of God was lost. Death entered the world and the world became worldly. Evil was now in the good creation, and it was also in the heart of people.

The revealed condition of the man and woman in Genesis 3 is a description of our lives to this day. The Word of God describes their situation after the fall into sin: "Then the eyes of both were opened, and they knew that they were naked. And they sewed fig leaves together and made themselves loincloths. And they heard the sound of the LORD God walking in the garden in the cool of the day, and the man and his wife hid themselves from the presence of the LORD God among the trees of the garden" (Genesis 3:7–8).

Everything had changed within their souls, and this is our condition as well. The first thing they did was realize they were not right. They were suddenly aware of their nakedness. For the first time, self-consciousness and self-condemnation filled them. No longer were they outwardly preoccupied with God and His love; now they were inwardly preoccupied with their condition without God. That's not the way they were created; that's not the way they were designed.

Now standing without God, they knew that they were wrong in their persons. Shame prevailed. Having lost communion with God, how could they be right? Their tether to life was cut off. They were floating out in space alone. Everything was all wrong. They knew it.

As a result, when they heard the Lord coming their way, they ran. Fear reigned in their hearts toward God. Shame and fear go hand in hand. Once there had been peace with God; now they didn't even want to face Him. God was to be avoided.

NOT JUST UNBELIEF, BUT FIGHTING AGAINST GOD

God, however, has a way of finding us. When He found them, they resorted to hostility and accusation. They cast blame. In doing so, they were also resisting the way of God. Instead of confessing, they were accusing. They were acting like their new father, not the heavenly Father. They became like the enemy who accuses, called "the accuser of our brothers" (Revelation 12:10). It wasn't enough to hide from God; they were now going against Him. They were fighting Him. So are we.

This unholy trinity of the world, the devil, and our sinful hearts is stacked against faith. It is no wonder we struggle so much for our faith to see through this culture. It is a culture that fights against faith both from the outside and from the inside. Does faith in the Lord Jesus Christ even have a chance?

My dad was a U.S. Marine in World War II. He served in the Pacific Theater as an amphibian driver. They were the ones that launched from the big Navy ships to assault the enemy shore. Once the amphibian was close enough, the Marines raided the beach. It was a horrific scene. Many Marines lost their lives before making cover.

Once when my dad's amphibian was approaching shore, one of his fellow soldiers panicked and jumped into the ocean. In his heavy gear, he began to drown. My dad jumped in after him. Once my dad reached him, though, the drowning soldier resisted. Now they were both in danger of going under. My dad struck him hard enough to knock him out. Only then was he able to get him safely back to the amphibian.

PUT TO DEATH SO THAT WE CAN LIVE

The world and the devil bombard us and fight against our faith in Christ. And then the Lord comes to our aid, and we make it worse: we fight Him; we resist Him. The Lord then does something we might not expect. He takes this one making it worse and slays him. And in this case, He lets us drown. Then, with His almighty power and in the most tender mercy and love, He takes the one who is drowned and brings him back to life; He raises us from death; He gives us a new life. We are "born again," "born of the Spirit" (John 3:3–7). We cross over from death to life (John 5:24). The water containing the Word in Holy Baptism drowns the old rebellious life, it saves (1 Peter 3:21), and it raises a new person at the same time. We die and rise all in the same event.

In other words, on our own, yes, the situation is positively dire. On our own, faith does not stand a chance. On our own, forget about it. Game over. We can't muster faith in the face of the world, the devil, and our sinful nature. This is an impossible situation. But the good news is that God intervenes. God breaks through. God comes into our lives through His Son and through His Word.

The challenge is that it is so incredibly easy for us to forget this truth: that the Lord comes for the overwhelmed. Jesus reaches out His hand to grab the drowning sinner. We forget. That's what our sinful nature does to us. It causes us to forget and to look elsewhere for meaning and salvation. What the world, the devil, and our sin have in common is that they engage in the same chaotic strategy: get life to seem so crazy that we no longer see the Lord.

We get way too distracted. We start lusting for the things in the world, we start listening to the father of lies, and we naturally fight against God. Then Jesus comes. He comes through His Word and Sacraments. Through these Means of Grace, He slays the resisting sinner, and He raises up a new creation. In this rescuing work, real faith is given.

This faith—empowered by the grace of God in Christ— knows the Lord, accepts the Lord, and trusts in the Lord. It is a living faith. And this faith is equipped so that the saved sinner may sing the hymn and mean every word: "I once was lost but now am found, Was blind but now I see!"

This seeing is effective. This faith sees through darkness and clouds. It sees with understanding. It is fitted with the Word of Christ. It is like receiving brand-new lenses for the eyes. Once we just couldn't see. There was no way to focus, but with this faith, with God's lenses, we see.

We are going to look at several lenses of faith that work in complementary fashion, but first we need to take a new inventory. We have taken stock of the side that gets us down: the world, the devil, and our sin. Now we need to look at our new identity. It is exciting. It is a status that knows a new life. It *is* a new life. We should be fully aware of it. We should know it well. It is a status that has faith to see through the culture. It is a status with the right lens to see.

STRUGGLING ON THE INSIDE

UNCOVER INFORMATION

1. How would you define *contentment*?

2. In 1 Timothy 6:6–7, St. Paul connects godliness with contentment. What is *godliness*? Consider 1 Peter 2:11.

3. What is another way of referring to *original sin*?

4. What does God do to a person when he or she is baptized?

5. At the end of the day, what are the world, devil, and sin trying to accomplish?

DISCOVER MEANING

1. Beyond a bare definition, what does *contentment* look like?

2. Why do you think St. Paul connects godliness with contentment?

3. Not only does original sin represent the tendency to hide from God, but what does a person naturally do even after God finds him or her?

4. What does God slay—put to death—in Holy Baptism?

5. God's response to what tries to overwhelm the Christian is to give His Means of Grace. How might this fact impact the way Christians view attending church services?

EXPLORE IMPLICATIONS

1. If one is not content, how might this impact a person's faith?

2. We properly emphasize God's grace, but "being godly" implies action. How then should the Christian live?

3. Original sin leads to experiencing guilt, shame, and fear. If God's solution to these is rejected, what do you think a person will do to try to cope?

4. In Holy Baptism, a person is "born again," "born of the Spirit" (John 3:3–7). What marks this born-again life? What characterizes it?

5. The great hymn *Amazing Grace* sings, "Was blind but now I see!" What does this kind of seeing imply?

CHAPTER 3

REALITY CHECK—
CHRISTIAN

All that we covered in the first two chapters is true, but it isn't everything. There is a lot more to the story. Jesus Christ completes it. Better said, Jesus Christ completes us. Reality is incomplete; life is not fully realized without knowing what Jesus Christ has done (and continues to do). Life without Jesus Christ is like going through a frightening storm without seeing the ensuing magnificent sunrise with a glorious rainbow thrown in. Imagine thinking that the dark storm was all there was; imagine going through life never knowing what would follow. Scripture mentions the woman who forgets her anguish in childbirth for the joy that her baby has come (John 16:21). To know Christ is to receive the basis for forgetting our anguish and having it replaced by joy.

THE GOOD NEWS OF THE GOSPEL

This reality check, however (if we would know reality), comes with the caveat that we hold to the saving Gospel of Jesus Christ. *Gospel* is one of those words thrown around a lot. We need to know what it means. *Gospel* means "good news" or "glad tidings." It is a militaristic proclamation of victory by humanity's Champion and substitutional Representative over sin, death, and the power of the evil one. Jesus won a war for us. The Gospel announces that God has defeated sin and death for us through His Son.

Our death has been defeated. All that sought to destroy us—physically and spiritually—has been overcome by the Savior of the world, Jesus Christ. This Gospel "is the power of God for salvation" for all (Romans 1:16). It is the Good News that means God has rescued us from all that causes suffering and strife; it is the Good News that announces the forgiveness of sins, life, and salvation.

This is the Good News that all the stuff that gets us down— the evil in the world, the devil who accuses, and our sin from within—is overcome. They still confront us, but no longer do they have the last word in our lives. The last word is now Good News, the Gospel. This Good News proclaims that the universal predicament called "death" has been solved through the One who overcame death when He rose from the grave. This victory of life has been transferred to those with saving faith in this Gospel. This faith itself is created by God through the Gospel.

SAVING FAITH CREATED

Sadness is overtaken by the Good News. The Good News creates joy. In a profound and divine way, God creates a deep trust in the heart that in Christ He is now gracious toward us. This is what the Holy Spirit does in those who receive the Gospel. He forms in us what is like a spiritual organ called *faith*. A physical heart pumps blood; a spiritual faith pumps trust in Jesus Christ. Faith overtakes unbelief. Anguish is replaced by confidence that God is on our side. This is what God creates in people through the Gospel, and this faith in Jesus knows that death is conquered, and if the worst cause for sorrow and distress is now defeated, then what is left to overtake joy?

This creation by God called faith can never be reduced to mere head knowledge. God-created faith is transformative. It changes people even as those same people retain their sinful nature so that there is not just the old sinner but now also a new person simultaneously. Faith daily counters the sin that resides in the converted person. Martin Chemnitz gives a complete view as to what saving faith is. The following is a paraphrase of his five points:

1. Knows God's universal grace for sinners through Christ.

2. Assents to this universal grace applied personally to oneself.

3. Desires this grace out of feeling sin's great burden; seeks and prays for God's help through the benefits of the Gospel of Jesus Christ.

4. Trusts that the benefits of the Gospel have been personally received through God's Word and continues to trust even in the face of great trials and burdens.

5. Experiences "the joy of the Spirit" so that one feels "the new life and joy in God, happily rest[ing] in the promise of grace, even under the cross."[4]

Michael was a parishioner who wasn't coming to worship. He was an inactive member whose mother—a devout member in my parish—reminded me that he was also the focus of her intercessory prayers. Like a good Christian mother, she also encouraged me to reach out to her son. He had recently resigned his commission as an officer in the U.S. Navy, but even before that, he had fallen away from regular church at-

4   Martin Chemnitz, *Loci Theologici II*, trans. J. A. O. Preus (St. Louis: Concordia Publishing House, 1989), 502.

tendance. I was delighted when he took me up on my offer to meet at a Mexican restaurant. I like this approach for getting together. One might hesitate to get together with a pastor in general, but if a free Mexican lunch is thrown in, the chances of having an evangelistic encounter increase exponentially.

The young man (about thirty years old) was ready to share his frustration with me. He was intelligent, philosophical, and a realist by nature. He was serious about the issue at hand. "Look, Pastor, I'm going to be honest with you." His eagerness to share his quandary wasn't hidden: "I don't know how some people do it. They tell me about how they believe, but there is nothing I can do to give myself faith. I've tried. It doesn't work. I can't produce faith in myself." His bold self-disclosure was so up-front and honest that the look on his face wasn't too expectant. What could I possibly say in response to this? His experience was irrefutable. He knew the truth. He could not believe. This wasn't mere opinion. This was a confession of a fact in his life. He concluded, therefore, that he wasn't meant to have faith.

He had seen the "evangelists" who went to great lengths to position people for what he viewed as sophisticated manipulation in God's name. He had heard all the clichés about opening one's heart and making decisions for Christ. All these fell flat in his view and left him cold. Every time he considered deciding for Christ, he was immediately confronted by his doubt. He sensed that any effort he might make to go along with accepting Christ would be half-hearted at best or hypocritical at worst. Michael wondered whether the entire faith enterprise was giving in to wish fulfillment. His skepticism toward those who claimed to believe wasn't mean-spirited, but if any of those claims were true, he concluded, then maybe God was against him. He seemed both agitated and concerned. I was thankful for his openness.

Michael wasn't prepared for my first words in response as one wearing a black clerical shirt and white collar. I looked in his eyes with a slight, compassionate smile and yet my voice was firm and decisive: "You're right Michael, you can't. What you've said is true; you can't produce faith." It is safe to say that Michael was all ears from that point on. When I was finished sharing the nature of faith and how it is given to people by the God of grace, he was overjoyed. I witnessed someone have an epiphany.

Becoming a Christian does not happen because we figure out a way to come to God; it happens on account of God coming to us. Faith is not our work. Faith is rather the work of God (John 6:29); it is generated by God; it is created and produced by God. It is given to those who receive God's Word and Sacraments. God had not been waiting for Michael to somehow build a bridge to Him, but God had built a bridge to Michael starting with his Holy Baptism.

Just when the crushing weight of the world, the devil, and the sin in our heart convinces us that we are helpless to do anything for faith to come alive, God confirms our suspicion and then turns the tables: "You did not choose Me, but I chose you" (John 15:16). That choosing is made known when Jesus Christ is given to us. This is when we become Christians.

People with a living faith in Jesus Christ were first called "Christians" in Antioch (see Acts 11:26). This is an exciting identification. It is powerful and profound. It means that we are Christ's. A Christian is someone who belongs to Jesus Christ.

A NEW STATUS, A NEW LIFE

When faith in Christ is known, this belonging to Jesus isn't in any way a violation of freedom. Much to the contrary, it represents the greatest freedom. To belong to Jesus Christ means that one is set free from the terrible burdens of the world, the devil, and sin. To be a Christian is to be enabled to truly live, to know a proper relationship with God and with other people. Such a life is a great reversal of the calamity described in Genesis 3: shame is replaced by forgiveness; running from God is replaced by seeking Him out; and hostility toward others is replaced by love for others.

The Christian has these new life parameters because they are, as Scripture teaches, "in Christ," a descriptor used almost two hundred times in the New Testament that is another way of saying "Christian." This, however, is not simply an assertion. It is something that happens. It is experienced. There is a time and a place when Jesus joins a person—when that person becomes a Christian.

That is, Christians experience a positional change in their life status. The Christian knows an objective occurrence, from once being apart from Christ to being one with Christ. The Christian is joined to Christ, and the Christian can identify when in time and space this occurred. This is confirmed by the Word of God itself. In this way, coming to faith in the Gospel is directly connected to having been joined to Jesus Christ. For the Christian, this is not theoretical or simply claimed; rather, it is something that God does in a real way in real time. All of this points to the great gift of Holy Baptism.

Little Sarah attended the Lutheran Day School I had the privilege of serving. Through the ministry of our school, many children from the community heard the Gospel in our weekly chapels, through the ministry of the dedicated teachers who taught the faith in their classrooms, and through my visitations to each classroom during the week. Sarah and her parents were not members of the church, but once Sarah heard about the gift of Holy Baptism, she went home each day begging her parents to let her be baptized. The parents couldn't take it anymore. Thanks to Sarah, they finally broke down and requested to see me. In my study, they asked me, "Pastor, what is required of us for Sarah to be baptized?"

Sarah sat there with her mom and dad, listening to me tell them the Gospel she had already heard. As it turned out, her father had never been baptized. That day in my study, arrangements were made for both dad and daughter to attend one of our Divine Services in order to be baptized. When the Sunday finally came, Sarah was going to burst with excitement, and her father was proud to be baptized alongside his little girl. His wife, Sarah's mother, stood by them to witness the very work of God.

THE NEW STATUS IS OBJECTIVELY VERIFIABLE: HOLY BAPTISM

This work of God occurs in history. It is objective. God attaches His Word to the water in Baptism, and Baptism through the water attaches God's Word to the person baptized. When this happens, the baptized is joined to Jesus Christ, the Word, who is God (John 1:1, 14). The position of the baptized in the universe changes. This baptized one is now in Christ; this one is a Christian. The new status means that whatever Jesus accomplished for salvation is directly applied to the baptized. Luther said, "[Christ has] through that same [water] placed heaven upon us and gives us the entire divine majesty as personally present and gives Himself fully and completely."[5] In this way, we are "baked into Christ. His death and resurrection are in me and I am in His death and His resurrection."[6]

Some of the most important Christian themes describe

---

5   Albrecht Peters, *Commentary on Luther's Catechisms: Baptism and Lord's Supper*, trans. Thomas H. Trapp (St. Louis: Concordia Publishing House, 2012), 89.

6   Peters, *Commentary on Luther's Catechisms*, 114.

something both *vicarious* (done for another) and *substitutional* (in the place of another). The idea of inheritance is also a vital part of the new life described in the Christian faith.

By being born, I entered my father's household. I was given his surname, I was granted the privilege of living in his house, and I benefited from what it meant to be a member of my family. As a child, I didn't pay for this. These things were given to me.

By being "born again," "born of the Spirit" (John 3:3–7) in Holy Baptism, I entered the heavenly Father's household. I was given a name: *Christian*. I was granted the privilege of living in the family of God, and I have benefited from all that Jesus Christ has accomplished for me (what He did for me and what He did in my stead). As a child of God, I didn't pay for this. These things were given to me. They are given to all who believe. They belong to the baptized into Jesus Christ!

BENEFITS RECEIVED BY BEING
PUT INTO JESUS CHRIST

What are some of those benefits now belonging to every Christian? They include things like atonement, propitiation, expiation, redemption, reconciliation, and justification. How can we be certain that these were done for us? Because Scripture reveals that Jesus has done these things for everyone. God's grace is universal, and it is this universal grace message that the Holy Spirit works through to create saving faith. When such faith is created, then that person is a Christian. Such a person has received the Word, and having received the Word, the person receives Christ. Having received Christ, then there is no doubt that this one now belongs to Christ. Now belonging to Christ, this person is fully—not partially—and 100 percent a Christian. As much as we contribute to come into our earthly families, we contribute even less to come into the family of God. This is God's work and God's grace. This is what is freely given in the name of the Lord Jesus Christ. Let's consider what Christians have received.

ATONEMENT

Jesus Christ has atoned for the sins of the world. This is nothing about potentiality. It has happened. It has been accomplished. *Atonement* has a double meaning. It means "to cover" and "to be made one with." A great way to remember its significance is *at-one-ment*. But what is the object involved here? What is covering? What is being made one with us? Answer: the blood of Christ. Christ's blood covers us. We are made one with the blood of Christ.

The cross of Jesus Christ is popularly misunderstood. Many people have no clue as to its significance. Why was He crucified? Some view it as simply confirming a great miscarriage of justice. Some might go further: Jesus' cross is a symbol of His sacrificial love. It is that, but not merely that. Not even close. To say that Christ's crucifixion is just about ethical meaning falls way short of its real meaning.

As a first step for understanding the significance of the blood of Christ, we need to go back to Old Testament foundations about the application of sacrificial blood in general. Leviticus 17:11 helps us see the significance of blood: "For the life of the flesh is in the blood, and I have given it for you on the altar to make atonement for your souls, for it is the blood that makes atonement by the life." Life is in the blood.

This is an important first step for any discussion about the importance of what Jesus Christ accomplished on the cross of Calvary. Otherwise, the entire discussion seems random. Why all this attention on His shed blood on the cross? Why is so much attributed to His blood for us? It is because sinners are overwhelmed by the penalty of sin, which is death. We are confronted by death. Regardless of how anyone might argue whether or not they need the saving faith, they must still deal with this terrible problem called *death*. This is the universal malady, the universal problem. What can we do about it? There is only one counterpower.

Atonement in the Old Testament was the fundamental answer to sin. It was the central reason for animal sacrifices, which pointed to the greater sacrifice that would be made by the Messiah, the coming Christ. The curse of death, the result of sin, had to be dealt with. Death would be covered by life. The great virus that kills would receive a greater virus to kill it. People marked by death would be covered again by life. Atonement brings life. That's why Jesus came. He said, "I came that they may have life and have it abundantly" (John 10:10). When He shed His blood on the cross, this was for the sin of the world. The New Testament unravels exactly how His blood brings life. Through faith in Jesus Christ, this gift won for the world is also the great gift celebrated by every Christian in personal possession of it.

PROPITIATION

Propitiation is "the turning away of wrath." People struggle with this. "If God is love, then how can we speak of His wrath?" We need to be a little more thorough in our analysis. If a man loves his family and comes home to find a thief or robber trying to harm his family, what does his love compel him to do? He does not start a negotiation. If a woman is pushing her baby in a stroller along a sidewalk and someone tries to take her baby, what does her love compel her to do? She doesn't invite the perpetrator over for coffee.

Sin came around as an archenemy to kill God's beloved people. The God of love would not stand idly by. God loves all people. He sent Christ to die for all people. Sin had to be dealt with. Sin itself provokes wrath, because God hates what is against His beloved. We are commanded to love (John 13:34), and as we cling to what is good, we are also commanded to hate what is evil (Romans 12:9). God loves us, so He hates whatever tries to destroy us. Love cannot be "sanitized" so that it does nothing in the face of evil.

Sin, however, is not abstract. It is found within people. From our limited perspective, how does God deal with sin while it is stuck within people? Here's another way of putting this question: How does God hate the sin and love the person at the same time? His way is by sending Jesus Christ.

The wrath of God was poured out upon our sin while it was no longer on us. It was put upon Christ. "For our sake He made Him to be sin who knew no sin, so that in Him we might become the righteousness of God" (2 Corinthians 5:21). We did not have to suffer that wrath upon sin, because Jesus deflected it from us. Jesus absorbed it for us. God's wrath toward us was, in other words, appeased. This is propitiation. His wrath is satisfied. He dealt with our sin without harming us. As for Jesus, this is something He chose to do for us. He wanted to do it. He loved us and loves us that much, and the heavenly Father loved and loves us that much. He was willing to give up His Son for us.

Now sin—all sin in all people—has been dealt with. The punishment of sin, the wrath poured out upon it, has been conducted. It's done. It's over. Jesus said, "It is finished" (John 19:30). This is what Christians trust in, and it is this faith—created by God through the Word—which assures the Christian that all his or her sins are forgiven by God. "[Jesus Christ] is the propitiation for our sins, and not for ours only but also for the sins of the whole world" (1 John 2:2).

EXPIATION

One result of propitiation is *expiation*, and this is how the same Greek word for *propitiation* is sometimes translated. Expiation is another angle of propitiation. As far as God is concerned, now that His Son, our Savior, has done what He has done on the cross, the guilt of our sin is gone. We have been cleansed, we have been washed, and our sin has been blotted out. Sin and its guilt are removed. Our sin has been expiated by the blood of Christ. Henceforth, as we live in faith in Jesus, God doesn't see our sin anymore. In His eyes, it's gone and forgotten by Him. This is the confidence of the Christian. It is affirmed by God's Word. While John 1:29 does not use the Greek word translated as "expiation" or "propitiation," it nevertheless puts forth a similar idea: John the Baptist said of Jesus, who was coming his way, "Behold, the Lamb of God, who takes away the sin of the world!"

Already in the Old Testament God revealed this attitude within Himself toward sinners, as Jesus—the answer to our sin—was the Gospel in place even "before the ages began" (2 Timothy 1:9). God revealed centuries before Christ was born, "I, I am He who blots out your transgressions for My own sake, and I will not remember your sins" (Isaiah 43:25).

This is a deep mystery. God is omniscient. He knows all things. How does He, how can He, possibly forget? He chooses to forget because of His Son, Jesus. Furthermore, legally, He can and should forget, because His Son bore our sin. His judgment against sin was satisfied by the sacrifice of Jesus. Sin having been dealt with, it no longer bears guilt upon us. It is now easy for God to forget.

That's why God's Holy Absolution—whether applied in the general, public Divine Service or individually in a private setting—is so powerful. God assures us personally of His great forgiveness and its quality: divine forgetfulness. When a person receives absolution, God is declaring that the sin forgiven is the sin forgotten. On one occasion, a parishioner sat in my study, having received my stole around his neck and my thumbnail sketch of the sign of the cross upon his forehead, and having heard the words "As a called and ordained servant of Christ and by His authority, I therefore forgive you all your sins in the name of the Father and of the Son and of the Holy Spirit. Amen." When my parishioner stood after the short service and asked, "Now that I've been forgiven this terrible sin, what now?" I replied in the spirit of what had just happened, "What terrible sin?"

REDEMPTION

Recall that we considered what confronts us from the outside and from the inside, namely from the world, the devil, and our sin. Jesus said plainly, "Truly, truly, I say to you, everyone who practices sin is a slave to sin" (John 8:34). Furthermore, in sin we were once captive to the devil to do his will (2 Timothy 2:26). We were enslaved. We were in prison. God sent His Son to redeem us, so Jesus came to pay a ransom to God Himself so that we would be released from slavery, released from spiritual prison. In this, we are given back to God. This rescuing work of Jesus is called *redemption*. Christ's atonement, propitiation, and expiation for us on the cross also secured our freedom.

The Gospel of St. Mark records these words of the Lord Jesus describing His own ministry: "For even the Son of Man came not to be served but to serve, and to give His life as a ransom for many" (Mark 10:45). Jesus refers to Himself as the "Son of Man" because in coming to take on human flesh and become man, His ministry was for the salvation of all men (male and female). This giving of His life *bought back* our lives from death to life, from enslavement to sin to freedom from sin. He paid this ransom to the heavenly Father, and this led to our liberation from sin and the evil one.

As I said before, these forces still harass and encumber us, but they no longer define us. These do not own us. These are not our masters. We are released from their enslaving power. We are now free to serve God. Having been redeemed by Christ, the curse of sin is no longer upon us. "Christ redeemed us from the curse of the law by becoming a curse for us—for as it is written, 'Cursed is everyone who is hanged on a tree'" (Galatians 3:13). Christ took our curse, and having bought us back to God, the curse is removed. We're free.

RECONCILIATION

The work of Christ also ushers in a new relationship with God. Being covered by life (atonement), having God's judgment and wrath appeased (propitiation), having the guilt of sin removed (expiation), and being set free from the enslavement of sin and the evil one (redemption) all impact our standing before God Himself. Once there was hostility between God and man (recall how Adam and Eve ran and hid from God and then resisted His invitation to confess, and chose hostility instead [Genesis 3]). Now there is reconciliation.

St. Paul describes this new status: "For if while we were enemies we were reconciled to God by the death of His Son, much more, now that we are reconciled, shall we be saved by His life. More than that, we also rejoice in God through our Lord Jesus Christ, through whom we have now received reconciliation" (Romans 5:10–11). If God would do all of this for us while we were still His enemies, how much more will God do for us now that we are His friends?

We are no longer separated from Him. No longer alienated. We are now reconciled. We are now back together with God and in His good graces. All of this describes the Christian's new identity. The root cause of our separation has been put away and the bridge between God and man is open. We are now right with God. How much more will God do for those in fellowship with Him? We are unable to describe the blessings of this new status.

JUSTIFICATION

Christians, though, still have a sinful nature, so it is easy for us to experience doubt. In a way, therefore, we are saving the best for last. All that we have described is outside of us. It isn't true because of anything we do or feel or think; it does not rest upon our prayer, our sincerity, our spirituality; and in no way, shape, or form does it depend on our personal conviction, decision, or assent. It is objectively true apart from us. It is forensic and possesses legal objectivity. We are declared by God to be righteous. What moves God's legal judgment to pronounce us righteous and not guilty? Jesus is the answer. God declares us righteous because of His Son. This is *justification*.

This is another way of describing the Gospel. It is about what Jesus has done for us to defeat the world, the enemy, and our internal sin. This Good News in and of itself leads to the creation of faith in our hearts. When people trust in this Good News for them, that God in Christ declares them forgiven, then they are personally justified. When objective truth (external) takes on the form of subjective faith (internal), then personal benefit is derived. The people with such a faith in God declaring us righteous by His Son are now justified. They receive the legal declaration from God that is the exact opposite of the word of condemnation. This is the word of justification. It is 100 percent certain for all that Christ has done.

St. Paul teaches about this justification: "Who shall bring

any charge against God's elect? It is God who justifies. Who is to condemn? Christ Jesus is the one who died—more than that, who was raised—who is at the right hand of God, who indeed is interceding for us. . . . [Nothing] will be able to separate us from the love of God in Christ Jesus our Lord" (Romans 8:33–34, 39). The answer to Paul's rhetorical question, of course, is that no one can condemn us anymore. God has justified us. St. Paul ensures that we understand that this justification is completely apart from anything we do: "And to the one who does not work but believes in Him who justifies the ungodly, his faith is counted as righteousness" (Romans 4:5). Note how in coming full circle, the concept of covering is connected to the verdict of justification: "Blessed are those whose lawless deeds are forgiven, and whose sins are covered; blessed is the man against whom the Lord will not count his sin" (Romans 4:7–8; see also Psalm 32:1–2). God doesn't count our sins anymore. They are covered; His wrath is appeased; the guilt, removed; the ransom, paid; reconciliation, achieved; and so there is now the declaration "Not guilty!" This is what the Christian knows and this is what makes a Christian a Christian.

Yes, we are up against so much in our lives. The world and the devil seek to discourage us and overwhelm us; and our own internal condition, our own sin that daily accuses us, can feel overwhelming. God, however, has not stood idly by. He has given to us the rest of the story. There is more to reality, and this reality check says that in spite of all the junk against us, there is a love and mercy in Christ that far, far outweighs the bad. God doesn't wait for us to pull ourselves up by our own bootstraps. He sends Jesus to do the work only He can do. He makes us Christians. We have a new status. God is on our side. There is more living to do and it's all good.

I was in the hospital room to comfort my parishioner, my brother in Christ. Mike was a joyful Christian. He was the real deal. He stood by my side at many midweek services to sing God's praises. He was a blessed cantor, and he had a passion for being in the Word of Christ. The medical report came swiftly. Even now, I marvel at how fast things went.

We learned of the grave concern by Mike's doctors, and I think he knew there was something wrong. But I look back in amazement. I was there to witness his split-second reaction when the doctor informed him of his terminal cancer and that he didn't have much time. Without missing a beat, he turned to me and locked eyes: "Well, Pastor, we have work to do. We need to make sure that all of my girls [his daughters] are in church and right with God." Not only was Mike not afraid of death, but all he cared about was that his faith would continue to be expressed even in the face of terminal cancer. Who or what could condemn him? Answer: nothing, but nothing. Mike was alive in Christ. His words echo in my ears many years later: "It's all good."

To be a Christian also means to be a disciple. In a way, they are synonymous words, but there is a little more to take into consideration. After all, God wants us also to know how to live in our culture. He has called us to live in faith. We are not Christians to hide our faith, but that our faith may be known.

REALITY CHECK—CHRISTIAN

Uncover Information

1. Define *Gospel*.

2. The Gospel does not only proclaim what Christ has done. What does the Holy Spirit create through its proclamation today?

3. Define *atonement*.

4. What does *propitiation* turn away from us?

5. The remaining benefits of Christ for us include *expiation, redemption, reconciliation,* and *justification*. Which one of these is least understood, in your opinion?

Discover Meaning

1. How does the fact that the Gospel announces a war victory help to understand it?

2. In your own words, summarize Chemnitz's five-point summary of what faith is.

3. According to Leviticus 17:11, what does blood contain?

4. If God truly loves us (and He does), how does He react toward anything that would try to destroy us?

5.   Isaiah 43:25 proclaims that God blots out our sin and doesn't remember it anymore. This helps us to understand the significance of expiation. Discuss how important this idea is for properly understanding the Gospel.

EXPLORE IMPLICATIONS

1.   The Gospel is both *vicarious* (done for another) and *substitutional* (in the place of another). How do these works of Christ for us and in our place help counter guilt, shame, and fear?

2.   If faith is the work of God (and it is), how does this truth help anyone who is anxious about being able to *make* him- or herself believe?

3.   When we are baptized into Christ, we are covered by and made one with His saving blood. What does this mean for the Christian in the face of death?

4.   Where has the wrath of God gone? What does this mean for us?

5.   Justification keeps the Gospel objective and outside of people. This is true: God declares you righteous in His Son, period. How liberating is this truth?

CHAPTER 4

REALITY CHECK—
DISCIPLE

Every Christian is a disciple, and every disciple is a Christian. The terms are practically synonymous, but not completely. They are, however, complementary and in a very important way. For a Christian to be a Christian, the Holy Spirit must work through the Word of Christ to create saving faith in Jesus Christ. God calls faith into being just as He called light into being: "And God said, 'Let there be light,' and there was light" (Genesis 1:3). God speaks and things come into being. No Word, no light. No Word, no faith.

THE NECESSITY OF THE WORD

God must give us faith. If He does not speak it into existence, it will never come. Just as Lazarus needed Jesus to call him to rise from the tomb (John 11:43–44), we need Jesus to call us from spiritual death (Ephesians 2:1) to the life of faith. Luther taught about this work of the Holy Spirit through the Word, which is something only the Spirit of God can do:

> I believe that I cannot by my own reason or strength believe in Jesus Christ, my Lord, or come to Him. But the Holy Spirit has called me by the Gospel, enlight-

ened me with His gifts, sanctified and kept me in the true faith. In the same way He calls, gathers, enlightens, and sanctifies the whole Christian Church on earth and keeps it with Jesus Christ in the one true faith.[7]

When I met Paul, he was nothing but cordial and polite. He had just brought his wife, Susan, and their children to Divine Service. After walking them into the narthex, he shook my hand with a warm smile, turned around, and promptly made his way back out to the parking lot, got into his car, and started waiting for his family to finish the church service. I had a better idea that day why Susan had asked me to pray for her husband. She had tried to share her faith, but it fell on deaf ears. She had invited him to church many times, but to no avail. He was dismissive. It wasn't his cup of tea. It wasn't his thing.

I took the request for intercessory prayer for Paul seriously, and I started looking for an opportunity—by God's grace—to convince Paul to simply receive a thorough presentation on Christian doctrine. My approach was to share with him what I would normally cover in an adult instruction class, an overview of the fundamentals of the faith, which could lead to adult confirmation. My rationale to him was simple: "How could you reject what has never been properly presented?" Paul was open and decided to invite me to his and Susan's home for the first class. I was excited and Susan was hopeful.

When the evening came, we settled in his dining room and enjoyed some hot coffee and cookies Susan had prepared. We were all in a good mood. They were both generous hosts, and I was feeling rather enthusiastic about the evening. God had opened a wide door. It was Paul's first time to receive this instruction, and Susan was all set to get a refresher. This was just what the doctor ordered. Paul just didn't realize what he was missing.

---

7   SC II (The Apostles' Creed, Third Article).

The meeting was a disaster. I was reminded that every article of the faith, its every assertion, has basic presuppositions behind it. Paul was ready to test every single one. "But how does one know that?" "Why should that be the case?" "How can that be?" My nice, neat presentation wasn't going so well. It came off like a lead balloon.

I left the house humbled. Paul seemed to be feeling justified in his position. He had been willing to have the pastor come over—making his wife, Susan, very happy—but now he only seemed affirmed in his stance. Not only had I not made things better, but thanks to me, the situation was now much worse. What happened next was completely unexpected.

Paul had life by the tail, and the world was his oyster. He lived in a gorgeous city not far from the Pacific Ocean; he had a beautiful wife and children who loved him; they lived in a great house with a view to die for. He was educated, with an earned master's degree in mechanical engineering from a top university. He had a fantastic job, drove a great car, and didn't have a care in the world.

One night not long after we had gotten together, Paul got home from work, was beat from the day, and went to bed. Susan described his sudden seizure in the middle of the night as violent. He shook so much that he fell off the bed. The paramedics responding to Susan's 911 helped stabilize him as they rushed him to the ER. Susan called me the next morning with MRI results: the malignant brain tumor was advanced and Paul didn't have much time.

Later that morning, I visited the hospital. I cared about Paul and I went to him in Christian love to do whatever I could. My failed attempt to present the faith was a thing of the past. All that mattered now was to support the family as best I could. Still, I wasn't quite prepared for my welcome when I arrived in his room. Paul was alone and his bed was angled so that he instantly saw me walk up to his door. The moment he saw me, he started laughing. Laughing hard. I stood there somewhat perplexed and awkward, but Paul explained his reaction: "Oh, Pastor, if you think I'm changing my mind about God just because of this, you've got another thing coming."

It was one of those moments in life when whatever was said next might determine the future of the relationship. To this day, I don't know where the words came from that formed my instantaneous reply: "Well, Paul, the way I see it, you're going to have a lot of spare time on your hands. We may as well make the most of it to get into your concerns about the Christian faith. Besides, talk about a perfect excuse for our hanging out at your favorite Mongolian restaurant."

Paul smiled, but I could tell he took me seriously. I believe he knew I was sincere. He could see that I cared. I also knew what Paul needed. Someone needed to treat his objections with respect and thoroughness. He needed thoughtful responses. This was an occasion for Christian apologetics. Not that the apologetics in and of itself would convert anyone—no one ever came to faith because of an effective demonstration of the reliability of the New Testament manuscripts or a thorough outlining of historical evidence for the resurrection of the Lord Jesus—but these were rather the intelligent underpinnings for the transforming Gospel itself. Thomas did not reach out to touch a ghost. He saw and touched the risen Christ in real time and history, and he gave up his life for the testimony now recorded in sacred Scripture.

My plan was simple: I would give Paul the full attention his questions deserved and then, after each thorough discussion, I would share the Lord's Law and Gospel over and over again. He agreed to my proposal, and I couldn't help but wonder if he was envisioning skewering the pastor while getting free lunches.

We started our project, but what was really starting was the beginning of a wonderful friendship. This is what the love of Christ afforded. Paul was created, redeemed, and loved by God, and I had the privilege of getting to know him and simply love him. We started our weekly routine and, frankly, had a great time. We ate, conversed, laughed, and teased each other, and then we took walks. The walks were fantastic. Paul had his list of topics ready: the problem of evil, Christian exclusivism in the face of religious plurality, the challenge of neo-Darwinism, the claims about additional gospels and certainty of the canon. He had a long list of reasons for rejecting God's Word for so many years.

I'd like to say that my theological training for engaging on the topics was the key to what eventually happened, but it wasn't. The most important thing was love with the commitment to share the Word of Christ. By God's grace, the focus was the relationship even over and above the topics at hand, and, step-by-step, there was a simple witness to our problem of sin and the threat of death. Then we went on to God's answer to our problem by sending His Son, Jesus, to be our Savior from sin and death. That was it—over and over again over a period of months—and frankly, God took over. God was doing a work of creation that I could not see.

The day came when Paul was physically no longer able to go on those walks. Eventually, he was confined to a hospice bed in his home. By this time, after months invested in becoming friends, I was in the new routine of visiting my friend Paul and wrapping up our time together with prayer. We had agreed months before that even though Paul could not pray with me, he would allow me to pray aloud and even pray for him. The prayers at his bedside were short and sweet, and one day, there I was, wrapping up yet another visit of enjoyable conversation, some bad jokes, and mutual respect for each other. I was wrapping up as I normally did: "Well, bro, I've gotta run. It was great seeing you. Let me pray." With that transition, I folded my hands and bowed my head as I prayed from the heart. I was thanking God for His love for us in His Son, Jesus Christ.

In the middle of the prayer, I almost fell out of my chair. Out of nowhere and while my eyes were closed, Paul's big left hand was now covering my folded hands. My eyes burst open in total surprise. I looked at him. Tears were streaming from his eyes as he looked at me and said, "I believe." My prayer continued with thanksgiving for the gift of faith through the Word of Christ.

The next day, I came over again. Susan stood by his side, his little children got onto the bed with him, and the large stainless-steel bowl filled with water was on the bed as well. The words rang out: "Paul, I baptize you in the name of the Father and of the Son and of the Holy Spirit. Amen." Not many days later, at Paul's funeral, I preached the Lord Jesus Christ who made Paul a Christian by the power of His Word.

Disciples are Christians who receive the Word of Christ and who furthermore remain in the Word of Christ. Romans 10:17 says, "So faith comes from hearing, and hearing through the word of Christ." The disciple is a hearer of God's Word. Paul received the Word of Christ, was brought to saving faith by the Holy Spirit, and for the rest of his life remained in the Word of Christ. This was what also made him a disciple. Every true Christian who remains a true Christian also remains in the Word of Christ. Nothing else sustains faith.

This doesn't mean that the disciple lives a carefree life, nor does it mean that the disciple does not battle sin or live in the spiritual battle between the sinful nature and the born-again spirit. This doesn't mean that the disciple does not bear a cross or suffer. It does mean, however, that there is one identifiable steady experience, as long as saving faith in Christ remains: the Word of Christ is always a part of the disciple's life, the Law of God is always leading to the confession of sins, and the Gospel of God is constantly leading to the forgiveness of sins in Christ. Such forgiveness gives another life, countering the old—a life that produces the virtues supplied by the Holy Spirit, like love, joy, peace, patience, kindness, goodness, faithfulness, gentleness, and self-control (Galatians 5:22–23). These flow from the faith produced by God's Word.

Jesus said to His first-century disciples, "If you abide in My word, you are truly My disciples, and you will know the truth, and the truth will set you free" (John 8:31–32). Disciples abide in the Word of Christ and this reveals the practical experience the Lord permits in the life of His people. This daily habit is the real countermeasure against the onslaughts of the outer and inner struggle. When the disciple of Christ gains this insight, then the Scriptures do not appear hyperbolic about the disciple's reliance upon the Word, but descriptive of their real desire. The psalmist described his reliance upon the Word: "Your word is a lamp to my feet and a light to my path" (Psalm 119:105). It becomes a part of everyday life:

> Hear, O Israel: The LORD our God, the LORD is one. You shall love the LORD your God with all your heart and with all your soul and with all your might. And these words that I command you today shall be on your heart. You shall teach them diligently to your children, and shall talk of them when you sit in your house, and when you walk by the way, and when you lie down, and when you rise. You shall bind them as a sign on your hand, and they shall be as frontlets between your eyes. You shall write them on the doorposts of your house and on your gates. (Deuteronomy 6:4–9)

THE WORD CREATES, THE WORD PRESERVES

There is a reason for this. Part and parcel of the doctrine of creation is the doctrine of preservation. It is humbling to consider that just as the creation needed God's Word to begin, it needs God's Word to continue. The Word is both a creative and sustaining Word. For example, as much as I needed God's Word for my physical body to exist, I need God's Word for my continued existence. Scripture teaches a concurrence: "In Him we live and move and have our being" (Acts 17:28), so that apart from God's preserving and operative Word, we could not even move a finger.

The same is true about saving faith in Jesus Christ. As much as we need the Holy Spirit to work through it to create faith, we need God to continue to work through it to keep faith alive. That is, that which is the Means of Grace for our justification is the Means of Grace for our sanctification. On one occasion when Jesus was in the home of Martha and Mary, Martha was agitated because her sister would not help her with meal preparations. All the while, Mary was sitting at Jesus' feet, listening to His teaching and hearing His Word. Mary was, by the grace of God, being a disciple. That's what disciples do. When Martha complained, Jesus told her, "Martha, Martha, you are anxious and troubled about many things, but one thing is necessary. Mary has chosen the good portion, which will not be taken away from her" (Luke 10:41–42).

This is a powerful Scripture. Like Martha, we are anxious and troubled about many things. We want to know, "What can I do? What help is there?" God's answer is to take up the "one thing . . . necessary." St. Paul teaches that we should think about and practice the things of Christ (see Philippians 4:8–9). This is God's answer for daily life that feels the threats of the world, the devil, and our sinful hearts.

God's way, however, is amazingly liberating. There is only one thing needful, not many things. Our Christian lives as true disciples are empowered by the Word of Christ. That which creates faith is the first cause of everything else that comes from faith, like, for example, good works. This means that the disciples' preoccupation is not about what they do, but rather about what they receive. Receiving the forgiveness of sins, life, and salvation, which is what the Word of Christ delivers (since the Word gives Christ Himself), leads to the rest of what Christians do. Prayer, service, and witness, for example, do not come from our discipline to respond to God's love, but rather flow from the faith that God creates and sustains. This is the fundamental reason we come to worship and the basic reason why the historic liturgy is based on the Word of Christ. We come to church to receive the Word, and this Word sustains and strengthens faith. This is the life of the disciple. Everything else that faith does follows this singular activity, which is not the work of man but the very work of God. This is the first stanza of the hymn "One Thing's Needful":

> One thing's needful; Lord, this treasure
> Teach me highly to regard.
> All else, though it first give pleasure,
> Is a yoke that presses hard!
> Beneath it the heart is still fretting and striving,
> No true, lasting happiness ever deriving.
> This one thing is needful; all others are vain—
> I count all but loss that I Christ may obtain![8]

It's true that *Christian* and *disciple* are two words that are practically synonymous. Indeed, to belong to Christ—to be in Christ—is inherently to be a disciple of Christ. Let us, however, be clear: the disciple of Christ is one who knows this one

---

8   *LSB* 536:1.

thing needful; the disciple is perpetually in the Word of Christ. The disciple is specifically a hearer of the Word of Christ. This of course is what Christians are always doing, but in today's culture there are too many compromises. There are too many deceptive and lazy versions of what it means to be a Christian. No wonder we find ourselves unnecessarily struggling (the legitimate struggles are enough). Without the Word filling hearts and minds, there can be no lasting faith. Christians are therefore conscientious about being in the Word. They remain hungry and thirsty for the Word of Christ. This is what disciples do.

At the same time, to be a hearer of the Word is also to be a learner of the Word. There is one particular lesson that leads to joyous and considerate expression. Disciples, always receiving this Word, can't keep it to themselves. The Word overflows in their lives. Disciples share the Word, and this means that every Christian who is a disciple is also a priest. This is yet another way that the Lord has arranged to protect us from the onslaughts of the world, the devil, and our sin. Before we know it, we don't have time for these distractions. We have better things to do.

REALITY CHECK—DISCIPLE

UNCOVER INFORMATION

1. It is easy to treat *Christian* and *disciple* as synonymous terms, but what activity marks being a disciple? Please also comment.

2. How did Jesus draw Lazarus from the tomb in John 11:43–44?

3. Review Luther's words "I cannot by my own reason or strength . . . ." Who exactly calls by the Gospel?

4. According to Romans 10:17, from where does faith come?

5. How does the psalmist consider the Word in Psalm 119:105?

DISCOVER MEANING

1. Disciples are not constantly in this "one thing necessary" in order to look good or simply "act Christian." Why are disciples always engaging in their disciple activity?

2. By the same principle working in John 11:43–44, Jesus calls people to faith. When and how does Jesus do this today?

3. After the Holy Spirit calls by the Gospel, what else does He do for the Christian?

4. In spite of the ongoing struggles Christians face, what virtues or fruits of the Holy Spirit should the Christian expect to know? See Galatians 5:22–23.

5. Christians speak of "being in the Word." How does Deuteronomy 6:4–9 expand on this?

EXPLORE IMPLICATIONS

1. Disciples understand that the Word of Christ is crucial not only for creating faith but also for sustaining faith. Why then is it so hard to remain daily in the Word?

2. If Christ has already called us to faith through His Word, why do we continue to receive the Word over and over again?

3. Christian apologetics are valuable, but what is most important to share with people, and why?

4. In John 8:31–32, Jesus talks about a benefit of being a disciple in His Word. How would you put this benefit in your own words?

5. What might your Luke 10:41–42 discipline look like?

CHAPTER 5

REALITY CHECK—
PRIEST

I could tell that when my administrative assistant—also an active member in the congregation—came into my study, she had something on her mind. "Pastor, I have a favor to ask." She was a little reticent because she was about to make a request of me to serve someone who wasn't a member. "I have a friend up north whose little boy is in trouble. He has a rare cancer, and they're coming down to Children's Hospital to begin intensive chemotherapy. I know you'll pray for him, Pastor, but would you see him? I think they could use a visit."

THE MISSION TO SHARE THE WORD OF CHRIST

The Lord is an expert manager of His kingdom work. He connects His people to others so that the light of Christ, the saving Gospel, might be shared with as many people as possible, because He desires all to be saved and to come to the knowledge of the truth (1 Timothy 2:4). This is the work of the Great Commission of our Lord (Matthew 28), given to His Church on earth: to all the Lord's royal priests, men and women, boys and girls, who are also Christians and disciples called to share the Word of Christ.

I asked my administrative assistant some questions about the little boy. Billy was only eight, and while he had an incredible way of coping with his disease, he was getting tired and the prognosis wasn't good. The little boy was showing signs of real depression. He had been in and out of doctors' offices and hospitals way too often, and now the most rigorous part of his treatment was about to commence. I don't know why I asked, but I did: "Does he have a favorite superhero?" She smiled. "Does he ever, Pastor. He loves Batman!" I had some extra fodder for my upcoming visitation.

In preparation for my visit, I made sure I had my Bible and hymnal, but this time I packed a duffel bag. My talented wife made a terrific costume for me so that I could be the Caped Crusader himself. The mask was an incredible rubber rendition of the real McCoy (this part was store-bought), the utility belt she fashioned was the bomb, the suit was dark black, the army boots were a perfect match, and the cape was long and impressive. When I arrived at Billy's floor at Children's Hospital in my clerical collar, I simply asked the nurses if there was a room I could change in.

It took a while to get dressed, but about fifteen minutes later, the metamorphosis was complete. I was already 6 feet 5 inches and about 250 pounds. With the costume ears and the extra heel on the boots, I was an imposing Batman. I left the dressing room and started to walk across the hall to Billy's room. Halfway down was a nurse's station attended by two nurses. One was standing facing my direction and the other was speaking to her with her back toward me while sitting in a chair. The one standing spotted me and looked shocked. Her mouth gaped as she let out a gasp. Her co-worker, startled by the reaction, swung around in her swivel chair. When her eyes hit me, she fell off her chair. I hadn't meant to scare anyone. When the two nurses put two and two together, they couldn't stop laughing.

Billy's mother had prepared her son. He had a very special visitor today. It was someone he really liked, but he shouldn't be surprised; her son was that special. When I walked in, Billy was in a state of disbelief, but his sheer exhilaration took over, and Billy got into the moment: Batman had come to see him!

We had a great chat. We discussed some of Batman's archenemies, the Batcave, and Robin, of course. He was thrilled when I presented a gift to him. It was a small Batmobile. He cherished it the moment I put it in his hands. At the height of Billy's enthrallment, I got to the most important part of my visit. Billy was genuinely surprised when his superhero confessed that he had a Superhero of his own, one that was the most important person and who was completely real.

Batman told Billy about Jesus while presenting a second gift: a crucifix. Jesus had won forever-life for Billy. Jesus was so great and so strong that death couldn't even beat Him, something that not even Batman could pull off. And Jesus was so real that whole churches throughout the world bore His name, and millions and millions of people followed Him. Jesus was the real Savior from all the bad things in life—even from the worst bad thing, called "death." Billy had nothing to fear. Billy was going to be safe. Jesus was protecting him every step of the way, and the coolest thing was that when Billy needed Jesus, there were no floodlights or bat signals to worry about. All that Billy needed to do was to call on His name. Jesus would be with Him always. Billy was so joyful at this news that I saw firsthand what the Gospel could do. Batman would have to take a back seat to the Maker of heaven and earth and the Savior of the world. He was glad to.

The family eventually traveled back up north after Billy's treatment, and then my administrative assistant close to Billy's family also moved away. I lost track of Billy. Years later, my old admin contacted me and asked if I would officiate at a relative's funeral. After the graveside service, as I greeted folks, I didn't expect to see Billy's mom. Even while she was still at a distance, my mind raced to know what to say. Assuredly, she was missing her little boy. She walked toward me with a smile on her face, and I felt humbled that the Lord had permitted me to serve her son. Her greeting was warm and sincere. She gave me a hug, then backed away, locked my eyes, and said, "Pastor, look!" She turned sideways and pointed toward Billy. He was running up behind her. I was speechless. For myself, I was experiencing a fantastic reunion, but as for Billy, he had never met me before. He remembered meeting someone much more exciting than me. That was okay, because this little one knew how much Jesus loved him.

WHEN ETERNAL LIFE BEGINS

When anyone comes to saving faith, they come into possession of eternal life. Eternal life does not begin at physical death, but at the moment we cross over from death to life (John 5:24) through faith in Jesus Christ. That means at conversion (when a person comes to saving faith in Jesus Christ), that person receives the greatest gift imaginable: life that doesn't end. Not just ongoing existence, but the guarantee that after death, exulting joy will fill the soul of those who go to be with God. Jesus called this state "paradise" while He was dying on the cross (Luke 23:43). The promise of eternal life gets even better, because following heaven is the resurrection of the body. Then comes the new heaven and new earth, when paradise will get better, the place that Jesus came to give to those who trust in Him.

This is good news, to put it mildly, and good news is meant to be shared. As a matter of fact, God has commanded that it be shared. He is that serious about the salvation of people confronted by the struggles from the outside and inside. God doesn't want anyone left out, and to prove His universal emphasis, He made sure that the Gospel itself—the Good News message—is clear that He loved the world and that His Son was sent to save the world (John 3:16–17). This world includes everyone. The Scriptures do not say that Jesus came for people *throughout* the world but for the *whole* world, every single person. God's grace is for everybody. The universal nature of this Good News proclamation itself reminds us why the Gospel is "the power of God for salvation to everyone who believes" (Romans 1:16). The Holy Spirit reveals that Jesus atoned for the sins of each one as well as for the whole world (1 John 2:2). This is one of the exciting realities of the Gospel: no one is excluded from the historical fact that Jesus died for each one to cover his or her sins with His blood.

One of my best friends loves to share the faith. He shares the Gospel boldly, lovingly, and personally. He was out and saw a homeless man. When they made eye contact, my friend said, "Jesus died to forgive you all your sins." The homeless man came back gruffly: "I don't believe in that stuff." My friend replied loudly, "Too late! Already done!" The homeless man started crying. He said, "No one has ever told me that before." The universality of God's grace is already established. All that is left is for us to believe what is already true and complete.

WHAT A PRIEST DOES

Every Christian, every disciple, has been given the privilege of sharing in this universal mission of sharing the Gospel. This adds one more dimension to our identity that counters the onslaughts of what tries to discourage us and bring us down: not only are we *Christians*—in Christ—with a new identity marked by what Jesus Christ accomplished for us (our atonement, propitiation, expiation, redemption, reconciliation, and justification); not only are we *disciples* given the constant pleasure of being in the Word of Christ that preserves and strengthens our faith in Him; but we are also *priests*. Yes, that's right, priests. A priest is someone who stands between God and other people. A priest talks to God about other people (in devout prayer) and talks to other people about God (in loving witness).

The words recorded in 1 Peter 2:9 reveal God's Word to the people of His Church (all Christians, all disciples) and not just a chosen few: "But you are a chosen race, a royal priesthood, a holy nation, a people for His own possession, that you may proclaim the excellencies of Him who called you out of darkness into His marvelous light." Those baptized into Christ, those abiding in His Word, are the same ones called "a royal priesthood" and are called to "proclaim the excellencies of Him who called [them] out of darkness into His marvelous light." To these same priests, God instructs, "But in your hearts honor Christ the Lord as holy, always being prepared to make a defense to anyone who asks you for a reason for the hope that is in you; yet do it with gentleness and respect" (1 Peter 3:15).

This is an enormously important Scripture about what the priest does. The priest is not an obnoxious pest, trying to shove the Gospel down people's throats. He doesn't walk around with a bullhorn, forcing the Word of Christ into unwilling ears. Instead the priest extends the love of God. Priests are extensions of God's attitude toward people. A priest is an ambassador of the God of love, who desires to communicate what people need to hear according to their immediate needs, be it His Law or His Gospel. They want to proclaim God's excellencies in conversation, especially when others might ask for the reason for their faith. When they answer, they do it with gentleness toward the one they're speaking to, but also with respect toward the Lord who oversees every exchange driven by faith and love.

What might move anyone to ask about a Christian's faith so that the Christian might also serve in this life as a priest? The answer is by living in such a way as to willingly give oneself to others through selfless service. Such a way is not a matter of discipline or forced piety; but this life flows from the Gospel itself. The words of 1 John 4:19 state simply, "We love because He first loved us." This is the life of faith: God's love given to the Christian, flowing over from the Christian into the lives of others. Christ Himself came not to be served but to serve (Matthew 20:28), and this is what Christians do in imitation of their Lord and Master. This imitation, however, is something flowing from the faith created and nurtured by the Gospel.

When this new life is in effect, it transcends a culture increasingly marked by self-centeredness, and yet it is a life that refuses to remove itself from the culture so that the love of God might be known within it. We live in a culture where "the love of many will grow cold" (Matthew 24:12), but the God of love leads His people to go the other way. To live in love is to live counter-culturally. This is a life that stands out. This life, however, cannot be forced. It is simply the life that results from faith. It is a life of love where faith is active in the good works that God has prepared in advance for Christians to do (Ephesians 2:10). Jesus said, "In the same way, let your light shine before others, so that they may see your good works and give glory to your Father who is in heaven" (Matthew 5:16). By being dedicated to serving others in their time of need, good works will shine and doors will open for speaking the Word of Christ.

GOD'S COUNTER TO THE WORLD, THE DEVIL, AND OUR SIN

With this trifecta identity of Christian-disciple-priest, we see how the Lord counters the world, the devil, and the sin in our hearts. The world tries to remove God, but as Christians we know that we are in Christ. The devil tries to drive us to despair, but as disciples we remain in the one thing needful—the Word of Christ—which protects us. Our own sin tempts us to live only for self, but as priests we grow excited about our great mission to show and speak the love of God to others.

The plan is simple. The best things in life are. God's Word is testimony to this. As profound as the Word of God is, it is also simple so that its greatest message can be grasped by a child. Unfortunately, we have the awful tendency to make things harder than they have to be. How often has the Church developed evangelism programs that make sharing the faith the single most intimidating thing a Christian could possibly engage in? How many Christians automatically associate the ability to share faith with the need to be exceptionally gifted or trained? This is simply not true. People have basic needs. They also have common problems, things that cause them to worry, and things that cause them to fear. People understand guilt and shame. Most importantly, people—all people—must face death. Given these basic needs and problems, it is also true that people—all people—would benefit immensely from God's answers to these. These answers are found in Jesus Christ. At the end of the day, priests are sharing the news about another Person, a wonderful Person, the King of kings, the Lord of lords, the Savior, Jesus Christ. Priests talk about Him.

The priest network was alive and well when Steve entered my life. The first priest involved in serving him was his wife, Alexis. The couple had been married for about five years. They were research scientists, passionate about life, in love with each other, and blessed in so many ways. They had been trying to get pregnant. Then, as is often the case, the intrusive and unwelcome news came out of nowhere: Steve was diagnosed with terminal cancer.

Alexis continued to show her husband unconditional love.

She was always there for him, and her approach for sharing her faith was reminiscent of the description in 1 Peter 3:2, how a godly wife draws an unbelieving husband through "respectful and pure conduct." She deeply desired Steve to know the love of God in Jesus Christ, but Steve had considered himself an intellectual. Faith didn't seem rational. He was unwilling to believe.

When the diagnosis came, however, Alexis shared her husband's condition with a friend at work. This friend happened to be a Christian and one who took her priesthood seriously. She comforted Alexis and committed herself to pray for Steve. She also asked Alexis about the kind of spiritual care she and her family had, and if they were currently being ministered to. When Alexis made it known that they didn't have a church home but that her background was like the tradition of my own parish, the Christian co-worker got Alexis's permission to phone my congregation, where we had an active prayer ministry. When the call came in, another Christian priest—the one who took the phone call at my parish—recorded the information and realized that Steve and Alexis lived in the same general area as one of our deacons. That Christian then took the initiative to phone the deacon.

The deacon—yet another faithful priest—gladly reached out to Alexis. When he did, he offered Alexis the services of our parish, and he made sure to tell her that the senior pastor (myself) was also available if Steve wanted to speak to him. Alexis happily passed these resources on to Steve. The deacon, of course, had phoned me as well. He knew he could always extend my service, but he wanted to be sure I knew what was going on. I was now also in the position to pray for Steve, a man I had never met. That, however, was about to change.

All of the people involved in this chain of events in service to Steve—from Alexis, to the friend at work, to the parishioner who took the initial phone call, to the deacon, and then to me—were Christians who understood their role as priests. We understood that God had made us conduits for connecting people to the Lord Jesus Christ, that we had been put on this earth for other people to know Jesus. Again, pretty simple.

Evidently, when Steve got the news from Alexis that my parish ministry stood ready to serve him, he was open to the possibility. Steve felt as though he was being urged to reach out to us. The day came when he decided to pick up the phone himself. He called me. I was happy that we set up a time for me to come to his home.

Steve and Alexis were the perfect hosts and nothing but welcoming. Steve's disease was at a stage where one would never know anything was wrong. We had a fantastic conversation in his living room. He was an extraordinary man. He was very smart and very friendly. The conversation was substantive and easy at the same time. It flowed. After a couple of hours, I felt as though I had known him for a long time.

Life had dealt Steve a hard blow, and so it was easy for him to ask the question. God's teaching in 1 Peter 3:15 about always being prepared to give an answer was being rolled out. Steve was asking me, and the ball was now in my court to speak to my new friend with gentleness and to respect and honor the Lord who had died and risen for Steve. The Lord was there and I had the privilege of telling Steve how the kingdom of God was already his through Jesus Christ. Life in the world had already laid on Steve the seriousness of the sin problem that leads to death, and the Holy Spirit had prepared Steve's heart to receive good news. I invited him to confess his sins and to receive through faith God's forgiveness and the gift of eternal life. To say that Steve was willing would be an understatement. The Holy Spirit was working powerfully in my new Christian brother's life.

Many more blessings ensued. One of those was his very specific prayer request. He and Alexis had just found out that she was pregnant. Their dream for a child was coming true. The problem was that his diagnosis gave him less time than needed to be able to meet his baby. He asked me to pray with him that he would be given more time. God gave him more time.

The time was also quality time in many ways. Alexis and Steve were now in the position not only to share their common love for each other but also to share their common faith. It wasn't enough for me to simply share the Gospel with him. Steve wanted confirmation classes. He wanted to become a member of the church. We were given time for that as well.

I will never forget that last day. Sometimes we get little inexplicable nudges. It was important for me to get up that early Saturday morning and drive into the city to the hospital where Steve was. I don't know why. I just couldn't go against conscience. I swung by to pick up one of our deacons and we were off. There was little traffic and we arrived quickly. When I walked into his room, it was still early, and so his wife and mom were both still asleep, all of them packed in the hospital room. Steve, though, was wide awake. He greeted me with a warm, loving smile. We had become close and he had already been treating me as though I was no longer a guest but a good friend. We didn't say much that morning. There was a sense of timing in the air. I took his hand and started to softly sing what had become his favorite hymn, "How Great Thou Art." As I sang, he smiled. Steve was joyful. Halfway through, his eyes widened. I paused to awaken Alexis and his mother. They swiftly came to his side to hold him close, surrounding him with love. I started to sing again, still holding his hand. He took a deep breath and then exhaled as he looked up, eyes wide open. Our brother in Christ Steve knew exactly what was happening. He knew the Lord was with him. He showed me how every Christian should hope to die. He knew that he would continue to live.

I look back on the great relationship I was given with Steve, Alexis, and then also their beautiful son, Connor. It had been made possible by God's work through the priesthood, and now I look forward to seeing Steve again. I'm thankful that he permitted the ministry of the many priests God placed in his life. I am thankful that he became one himself who shared God's Word and love back to me and others. It's going to be good to see my fellow priest Steve again.

REALITY CHECK—PRIEST

UNCOVER INFORMATION

1. Define *priest*.

2. To whom and where does Matthew 28:19 command the disciples to go to make disciples?

3. According to John 5:24, when does someone come to eternal life?

4. What does "world" mean in John 3:16?

5. According to 1 Peter 3:15, what two things is the priest conscientious about while sharing the faith?

DISCOVER MEANING

1. What should a priest include in prayer? What should a priest include in conversation?

2. Matthew 28:19–20 is known as the Great Commission. Why would Scriptures like 1 Peter 2:9 and 1 Peter 3:15 take this commission as being given to *all* Christians?

3. If Christians have eternal life before physical death (and they do), what happens to this eternal life in them when they die? Consider Luke 23:43.

4. Given the meaning of John 3:16, why is "throughout the world" inadequate?

5. How does the Christian demonstrate gentleness per 1 Peter 3:15?

EXPLORE IMPLICATIONS

1. The words of 1 Timothy 2:4 and 1 John 2:2 should give great confidence to priests when they consider sharing God's love with anyone. How so?

2. Because the Church takes God's commission so seriously, she develops evangelism programs. How might these help? How might these hinder?

3. If the "payoff" of someone receiving the Gospel is eternal life and paradise, discuss the value of commitment to being a priest.

4. Given the meaning of "world" in John 3:16, what do priests know to be true about the people to whom they are speaking before they even utter a syllable?

5. When 1 Peter 3:15 mentions "respect," this is toward God. That is, the exchanges priests have are never just between two. How does this help the prospect of sharing faith?

CHAPTER 6

THE LUTHERAN LENS—
WHAT IS REAL?

After getting through seminary and all the reading that comes with it, I was ordained and started my first pastorate. It was during this season in life that I realized my physical vision wasn't what it used to be. I started wearing glasses not long after becoming a pastor. I had been introduced to the optometrist, which is to say I had been introduced to the phoropter, which sounds more like a dinosaur.

THE PHOROPTER: LENSES
THAT WORK TOGETHER TO SEE

Anyone who wears glasses is probably familiar with the routine. You place the bridge of your nose against a large framework with lenses. Then the test begins. The optometrist measures one eye at a time, testing various lenses on each eye while asking the patient to tell him which projection is clearer: "One or two?" "Three or four?" "Five or six?" As the patient narrows down the selections, acuity increases. Before long, the optometrist finds the perfect lens that will work with each eye, working toward a 20/20 result. The two lenses are coordinated, aligned, so that one can see.

Very often, the inherent challenge lies in the fact that the eyes do not match. Typically, one is weaker, the other dominant. Taking each measurement into consideration brings focus. In the meantime, how easy it is to get bogged down with blurriness, and if we never do anything about it, we start to settle for poor vision. That vision—or lack thereof—colors everything. Everything is affected. Everything is compromised.

TWO LENSES, DUALITIES, AND PARADOXES

We begin to realize that the child of God has two different sets of experiences. One set is composed of their confrontation with the world, the devil, and their own sin, but the other set consists of the comfort derived from being a Christian, disciple, and priest. This is a real paradox, a real duality. These side-by-side experiences represent two lenses through which life is perceived. Both sets, or lenses, need proper consideration, because both powerfully impact our lives. When we learn the significance of these side-by-side dualities, then all of life comes into focus. Based on the first five chapters, this is how the two sets of experiences, or lenses, line up:

We experience the world.	We experience our identity as Christian.
We experience the devil.	We experience our identity as disciple.
We experience our sin.	We experience our identity as priest.

Consider how the right-hand column will not permit the weaknesses of the left side to take over to cause permanent blurriness in life:

The world removes God.	The Word gives Christ.
The devil accuses us.	The Word sustains faith.
Sin says, "Live for self."	The Word says, "Live for others."

Along the way, however, other vision problems can develop. Some of them are worse than others. Some might require surgery. Bottom line: some threats to our vision require more attention than others. The same is true when it comes to faith seeing clearly through the culture. These considerations for balance are presented in God's Word as paradoxes or dualities, but if we are not aware of them, our attempts to live our faith will continue to result in confusion and blurriness. It's important to be aware of these for our faith's visual acuity.

THE LENS OF VISIBLE AND INVISIBLE

The first additional lens is exactly about how we see. Our minds go to what is most obvious: what we look upon physically. The problem, however, is that all creation is not merely physical. The creation includes what is visible and invisible. Creation consists of the physical and the spiritual. We can't go along with the assertion that "all that matters is matter."

Even from a purely philosophical perspective, what is real cannot be reduced solely to the physical. Our brains are magnificent electrical systems, but the resulting thoughts and feelings are those things of the mind. The brain and mind are related, but they are not the same. A neurosurgeon can operate on a brain, but therapists, pastors, and good friends help the mind.

In addition, we would never reduce reality in general based upon what we see. We can see tables and chairs. What we can't see is their molecular structure. As a civilization, we once thought that Newtonian physics explained how the world functions, but all of this had to be revised when Einstein introduced a new physics at the subatomic level. At this level, we can't even predict how electrons will travel, especially while we try to adjust the very concept of travel. The point is that our idea of physicality and how it behaves is itself unstable. What we want to be stable and predictable doesn't conveniently align with our expectations. In truth, at this level of creation, things seem to pop up out of nowhere. That is, what is real betrays an unseen reality.

SPIRITUAL AND PHYSICAL

Still, the examples of the unseen so far have been restricted to the philosophical and scientific, but we can't stop with these. Scripture—which is impressively trustworthy and reliable in countless ways—also reveals God's message to us about the creation: it includes the spiritual as well as the physical. To come to the point, there is a spiritual realm in addition to the physical realm. The problem occurs when we assume that all that affects us is purely physical, so that everything about our health, for example, boils down to our physical diet and exercise. Nothing could be further from the truth. The peace we experience or the lack thereof is also directly related to our spiritual life.

God's Word teaches that human beings are body and spirit. When death occurs, there is a separation of the body and spirit (all the more reason we look forward to the resurrection, when body and spirit will once again be unified). Until physical death occurs, we experience both the things of the body and the things of the spirit; everyone does. But God desires to make us increasingly aware of what we typically treat as a nonfactor. It is easy to live as though all that is real and important is purely physical, but this is a limited view. It is an unrealistic view. In fact, the most important things involve what is unseen.

St. Paul wrote as recorded in Ephesians, "For we do not wrestle against flesh and blood, but against the rulers, against the authorities, against the cosmic powers over this present darkness, against the spiritual forces of evil in the heavenly places" (Ephesians 6:12). *Heaven* has different meanings in Scripture. Depending on the context, it might refer to the cosmos—the universe—or it can mean being in the presence of

God, something we look forward to as Christians when we speak of "going to heaven." Here in Ephesians 6, however, it refers to the invisible realm that includes both good things (like holy angels) and evil things (like fallen angels/demons). The heavenly realm is an unseen spiritual realm. This realm has a real influence and impact upon our daily lives. The Lord Himself received help from angels after enduring His temptation in the wilderness: "Then the devil left Him, and behold, angels came and were ministering to Him" (Matthew 4:11).

Given these things, we can understand why St. Paul teaches, "For we walk by faith, not by sight" (2 Corinthians 5:7). These words come in the context of St. Paul teaching about our body-and-spirit dichotomy. Again, there is more to what is real than what meets the physical eye.

Learning this, we see that balancing the lenses of what is seen and unseen is vital for living out our faith. We've all heard the conventional wisdom "Don't judge a book by its cover." It is a truism that reminds us that what is before our physical eyes does not tell the whole story. This is always true. It is especially true when we contemplate the wisdom of Romans 8:28: "And we know that for those who love God all things work together for good, for those who are called according to His purpose." As true as this Word of God is, it can also be tough to swallow. God is certainly not calling what is evil "good," but it also teaches that God works good through all things, even things that are very bad. When we find ourselves in the middle of a storm, however, the ability to see the silver lining isn't easy. When we can only see darkness and pain, well, that is all we see. It is especially unwise, by the way, to spit out "all things work for good" when someone is in the middle of horrific pain. There is a time and a place for everything.

Yet, there is more that we cannot see based upon our natural senses. There always is. Not sometimes, but always. This is true even of those things most sacred, like the life of the Lord Jesus Christ and the life of His Holy Church. Three things especially stand out that demonstrate this "seen-and-unseen" paradox:

- Jesus' birth, life, and death on the cross
- The Holy Sacraments of the Church
- The life of the Christian in this world

THE LENS OF FAITH SEES GOD HIDING IN JESUS CHRIST

The life of our Savior was a phenomenal paradox. He was predicted in the Old Testament to be the all-powerful and gloriously coming Messiah. He would be the Ruler of nations and the Savior of the people of God. It is understandable why the people of Israel might have emphasized these predictors while less often emphasizing the other messianic prophecies about His being the Suffering Servant for the sake of His people. They had been under the rule of many foreign nations; they had been subjugated and caused to suffer so much that they wanted to highlight one set of prophecies at the expense of the others. They lost their lens of "both-and" and were staring only at the one. Not only did this skew their understanding of the Messiah, but it formed a host of wrong messianic expectations. Fundamentally, they expected Jesus Christ to be a political—or worldly—Savior. The people of Israel had been under the rule of Egyptians, Assyrians, Babylonians, Persians, Greeks, and Romans. Enough was enough already; "Come, Lord Jesus, and conquer our earthly enemies." As a result, and to many in Israel, Jesus Christ was a complete and utter disappointment.

From this limited perspective, we can understand why the

birth and life of Jesus could not be fully seen and realized. Being born in a stable isn't exactly what we would expect for royalty. And while we might enjoy singing the Christmas hymn "Away in a Manger," it is fairly unrealistic that the infant Christ did not cry. If He was truly human—and the divine Christ was also that—then He would need to clear His lungs in order to breathe. He would have cried and engaged in all the other things little babies need to do, because as much as He was fully God, He was also fully human.

These humble circumstances would continue to mark His life. He was a carpenter's son born under the law (Galatians 4:4). For this reason alone, His blood was already being poured out when He was eight days old at His circumcision in accord with the Abrahamic covenant. Even after becoming a man and starting His earthly ministry, He continued to prove His humanity.

At the death of His friend Lazarus, He witnessed the great sorrow and heartache of those mourning, and as He contemplated these, He also wept (John 11:35). Such behavior did not seem fitting for the Son of God. Where was His power? One would think that after raising Lazarus from the grave, His skeptics might have come around, but then the day of His crucifixion arrived.

When the Lord Jesus was on the cross, the great temptation confronting Him was for Him not to go through with it. Jesus Himself had taught about His power, always at His disposal but held back due to His self-chosen limitation and humiliation: "Do you think that I cannot appeal to My Father, and He will at once send Me more than twelve legions of angels?" (Matthew 26:53). Still, the evil assaults came to try to stop His atoning work for humanity:

> And those who passed by derided Him, wagging their heads and saying, "You who would destroy the temple and rebuild it in three days, save Yourself! If You are the Son of God, come down from the cross." So also the chief priests, with the scribes and elders, mocked Him, saying, "He saved others; He cannot save Himself. He is the King of Israel; let Him come down now from the cross, and we will believe in Him. He trusts in God; let God deliver Him now, if He desires Him. For He said, 'I am the Son of God.'" (Matthew 27:39–43)

Many people—relying on what they saw and what they thought logically and reasonably—did not and could not see that Jesus really was the Son of God. They could not see that He was the Messiah. Nothing they saw could make sense of such a claim. He couldn't be. All they could do was reject Him. They were walking by sight. They were not walking by faith. The other set of messianic prophecies in God's Holy Word were being completely set aside. As a result of the Word neglected, many people could not see even when they were sure they could.

The hiddenness of God was fully active in Jesus. Yes, He wrought miracles, but He showed weakness and limitation. Yes, He claimed to be the Son of God, but He died a miserable death, and the Old Testament Scriptures declared, "A hanged man is cursed by God" (Deuteronomy 21:23). How could Jesus be the blessed one? What was seen and what was were two different things. It's true one really can't judge a book by its cover.

THE LENS OF FAITH SEES GOD
HIDING IN THE SACRAMENTS

The same is true as the holy things flow over from Christ to His Holy Church. The Lord chooses to bless His Church through His real presence given in, with, and under the blessed elements of the Sacraments. How can this be? How can such simple elements transmit such great and glorious blessings? How can mere water, mere bread and wine give the risen Christ? The glory of Christ and the outlandish simplicity of the natural elements do not align. What we see and what God says we receive appear contradictory at best.

Naaman was "commander of the army of the king of Syria, . . . a great man with his master and in high favor, because by him the LORD had given victory to Syria. He was a mighty man of valor, but he was a leper" (2 Kings 5:1). Naaman was a man of power and might, and his vision of anything great had to align with his idea of power and might. When he came seeking healing from the king of Israel, he brought with him ten talents of silver, six thousand shekels of gold, and ten changes of clothing (2 Kings 5:5). Great healing, in his mind, required great things. He did not expect that Elisha would say what he said:

> And Elisha sent a messenger to him, saying, "Go and wash in the Jordan seven times, and your flesh shall be restored, and you shall be clean." But Naaman was angry and went away, saying, "Behold, I thought that he would surely come out to me and stand and call upon the name of the LORD his God, and wave his hand over the place and cure the leper. Are not Abana and Pharpar, the rivers of Damascus, better than all the waters of Israel? Could I not wash in them and be clean?" So he turned and went away in a rage. But his servants came near and said to him, "My father, it is a great word the prophet has spoken to you; will you not do it? Has he actually said to you, 'Wash, and be clean'?" So he went down and dipped himself seven times in the Jordan, according to the word of the man of God, and his

flesh was restored like the flesh of a little child, and he was clean. (2 Kings 5:10–14)

Naaman was walking by sight, not by faith. It took the word of his servants to convince him to simply do what the Word of the Lord through the prophet said to do. He must have been amazed. How and why would the Lord do such a great thing through such simple and unimpressive means? And yet that is what God did, in spite of the fact that what happened did not align with Naaman's expectations—in spite of the fact that it did not match his sight. Faith had to take over to see what could not otherwise be seen.

In Holy Baptism, it is not the water that does great things, but the Word of Christ contained in the water; and in Holy Communion, it is not the bread and the wine that accomplish the forgiveness of sins, but the risen Christ who comes in, with, and under the bread and the wine. What we see is simple. What we see is not impressive. What faith sees, however, is everything. Faith recognizes the Lord when the Holy Sacraments are given and received.

THE LENS OF FAITH SEES GOD HIDING IN HIS PEOPLE

God is hidden in these Means of Grace, but He is still there. In fact, it is exactly where He promises to be. This, however, is not where the Lord's hiddenness ends, because He promises to abide in His people who receive His Word. However, consider these people: They are weak, they struggle, they doubt, they are often living and breathing in ways inconsistent with their confession. They do the things they know they should not do. They sin and they mourn. They die. How can these poor and heavy-laden ones be the very people of God? And yet, they are. God is hidden in them as they are made in the image of His Son, who also took on frail flesh.

It is easy to see a Christian and not be impressed. They are just people with all their frailties, with all their limitations. It is easy to only see that which is unimpressive and to assume, quite frankly, that there is absolutely nothing special about them. This, however, is not all reality, because these Christians are the ones in whom the Lord dwells. They are the ones promised the kingdom of God and they are the ones who shall be glorified. There is more than what the eyes behold. There is more behind the covers of these books. What is unseen far outweighs what is seen. St. Paul says, "For this light momentary affliction is preparing for us an eternal weight of glory beyond all comparison, as we look not to the things that are seen but to the things that are unseen. For the things that are seen are transient, but the things that are unseen are eternal" (2 Corinthians 4:17–18).

All of this means that we have the need to see rightly. The first step, however, is to understand that our first step in what we see has everything to do with how we see ourselves and how we see God. What we see first is not what God sees. Instead, as sinful people, we try to make what is into what it is not. Why? Because sin is always disputing God. Sin in people leads people to always contradict what God says.

THINGS ARE NOT AS THEY SEEM

Luther, in his Heidelberg Disputation, saw this contradiction, and what he wrote is true wisdom. Consider thesis 3: "Although the works of man always seem attractive and good, they are nevertheless likely to be mortal sins."[9] This is in contradistinction to thesis 4: "Although the works of God are always unattractive and appear evil, they are nevertheless really eternal merits."[10]

---

9   AE 31:39.
10   AE 31:39.

Luther, of course, was getting into the most important consideration of what is real and true, namely, the forgiveness of sins, life, and salvation. Man wants to believe (and does believe) that what he does is the basis for salvation; thus his works "seem attractive and good." However, to make this assertion is to deny God's way of salvation. This, of course, is a mortal sin since, in this case, actual salvation is patently rejected. On the other hand, when God establishes salvation through His Son, this is offensive to people. These "seem unattractive and appear evil," but the works of Christ are eternal merits, because His are the only works that save us.

What Luther was explaining is similar to the overall teaching of God's Word: "For My thoughts are not your thoughts, neither are your ways My ways, declares the LORD. For as the heavens are higher than the earth, so are My ways higher than your ways and My thoughts than your thoughts" (Isaiah 55:8–9). In addition, the Word of God in Proverbs states, "There is a way that seems right to a man, but its end is the way to death" (Proverbs 14:12). We don't *get* God's way.

When this revelation sinks into hearts and minds, then profound humility takes over. It is easy for us to no longer believe that we are as smart as we once thought we were. C. F. W. Walther is insightful about these things and offers a very practical analogy from the realm of higher education (in this case, for pastors):

> A godly Lutheran theologian once described students of theology this way: "When they get to college, they know everything. In their second year of study, they become aware of some things that they do not know. At the end of their last year of study, they are convinced that they know nothing at all." The lesson that the old theologian wished to convey is obvious: the worst delusion is to think that you have made tremendous prog-

ress in the acquisition of knowledge. As such, a sure sign that that person's knowledge must be very superficial is if he presumes to know a lot about his field. . . . The more truly learned a person is, the humbler he will become, for he knows how much he is still lacking, within what narrow boundaries his knowledge is confined, and how much still remains to be explored.[11]

THE THEOLOGY OF THE CROSS

Walther was prescribing humility, but this is not the way of human nature. Luther elaborated upon humility using yet another valuable lens for this discussion in terms of the *theology of glory* versus the *theology of the cross*. By "glory," Luther meant that people expect to see the work of God through things that are glorious and impressive in this life. These things are thought to represent great blessings from God that are obvious for all to see. By "cross," he meant those things very difficult to endure that cause suffering and pain. Nevertheless, Luther taught, the theology of the cross understands that God uses suffering and pain to bless and refine faith.

The theology of the cross is counterintuitive to people and seems repulsive to human reason. We must be careful to explain and not go in the wrong direction. Certainly, if what is understood by "the theology of the cross" is that suffering in and of itself makes us better and closer to God, then one *should* have a problem with it. Such ideas are reminiscent of penance, the idea that sacrificial works must be combined with confession so as to earn grace. Such ideas contradict Scripture itself. This is not, however, what "the theology of the cross" means.

The theology of the cross simply teaches that God hides

---

11   C. F. W. Walther, *Law and Gospel: How to Read and Apply the Bible*, ed. Charles P. Schaum, trans. Christian C. Tiews (St. Louis: Concordia Publishing House, 2010), 47–48.

Himself in ways of humility, quietness, and suffering in order to bless His people. These, however, are not self-imposed but are given by God. For example, if God gives holy matrimony, then the one who is faithful in marriage might be required to help his or her spouse through a serious illness or injury. If a husband or wife finds him- or herself serving a spouse through hard times, then that marriage involves a cross. In this case, suffering marks marriage, and if the couple are faithful, they will also be refined in their holy faith to God and in their holy love for each other. Such faithfulness is a great blessing in this life and the next (Revelation 14:13), but the world does not see much that is positive. In fact, some people might assume that this marriage is cursed. The theology of the cross, however, recognizes the beauty and power of God in such a marriage.

Jesus said, "If anyone would come after Me, let him deny himself and take up his cross and follow Me" (Matthew 16:24). The lens of faith learns to see that God is often working good when others think that there is only bad. Faith sees that following the Lord includes self-denial (when we would only live for self), but such self-denial does not come naturally, so the Lord helps by giving a cross. When we are faithful to that cross, the Lord uses the cross to bless our faith. This is not self-evident, but with the proper lens, we can see that suffering in this context of the cross represents the glorious work of God. It is a work that preserves our faith in this world, which seeks to rob us of faith; and it is a work that often forges us to be a blessing to others.

Luther was teaching about this biblical theology in his Heidelberg Disputation. First of all, "Man must utterly despair of his own ability before he is prepared to receive the grace of Christ" (thesis 18).[12] As a result, the *theologian* (the one who knows the things of God) begins deciphering between the

---

12   AE 31:40.

visible and invisible. Luther continued: "That person does not deserve to be called a theologian who looks upon the invisible things of God as though they were clearly perceptible" (thesis 19).[13] In other words, the invisible things of God are not visible to man. Luther asserted, therefore, at thesis 20: "He deserves to be called a theologian, however, who comprehends the visible and manifest things of God seen through suffering and the cross."[14] This, however, is not the natural inclination of people, since in suffering it is common to assume that God is far away. At thesis 21, therefore, Luther explained, "A theology of glory [which does not recognize the true work of God] calls evil good and good evil. A theology of the cross calls the thing what it actually is."[15]

The theology of glory relies on man's way of thinking. A theologian who embraces this notion behaves like Naaman, who insisted that what is impressive to man should be the way of God. The theology of the cross, however, does not assume that what people consider bad is always bad. Such a lens starts to see what others do not see. It sees that sometimes in terrible suffering, there is a totally undetectable good. Such a thought humbles us, because surely this is not what one would ever rationally anticipate. Nevertheless, consider this: In the single greatest moment of suffering in the history of humanity, the greatest blessing for humanity was accomplished. The only Innocent One was covering the sins of all people with His blood. At Calvary, what was visible was a Jewish man about thirty-three years old or so, helpless and dying in agony on a Roman cross outside the city gates of Jerusalem. Where was the power? What was the gain? What only faith could see, what only the theology of the cross could see, was that the Son of God was saving all people for all time from sin, death,

---

13   AE 31:40.
14   AE 31:40.
15   AE 31:40.

and the power of the devil, and was redeeming all people for all time through the forgiveness of sins, life, and salvation. The lens of faith sees what the world cannot.

This principle also applies to the life of the Christian. This is St. Paul's testimony of his own life:

> So to keep me from becoming conceited because of the surpassing greatness of the revelations, a thorn was given me in the flesh, a messenger of Satan to harass me, to keep me from becoming conceited. Three times I pleaded with the Lord about this, that it should leave me. But He said to me, "My grace is sufficient for you, for My power is made perfect in weakness." Therefore I will boast all the more gladly of my weaknesses, so that the power of Christ may rest upon me. For the sake of Christ, then, I am content with weaknesses, insults, hardships, persecutions, and calamities. For when I am weak, then I am strong. (2 Corinthians 12:7–12)

Whenever I've commenced a pastorate, one of the first priorities has been to find out about homebound members, members unable to attend the public services. I started to prepare to meet Henry and Grace Peterson. They were now well into their sixties and had been married for decades. They were deeply in love, and I must say that I've never seen a greater example of marital devotion and fidelity. It's been a long time since I served them, but their lives continue to inspire me.

The Petersons were living a wonderfully active life. They were not bumps on a log, but social and vibrant. Joy was theirs, and everyone they touched they blessed. Halfway into their storybook marriage, Grace was diagnosed with ALS, also known as Lou Gehrig's Disease. Grace had been living with the disease for many years when I met her and Henry. What I saw in them was mind-blowing. They were the epitome of the greatest example of holy marriage.

When we met, Grace was already at the stage that she was, for all intents and purposes, completely paralyzed from the neck down. Still, when Henry welcomed me into their home, both of them greeted me with big smiles and everything about them indicated they knew the Lord and loved His people. Grace was still full of life, wonderfully conversant, and unwilling to allow any disease to cripple her faith, hope, and love. One could tell after spending just five minutes with them that they were the real deal and that they loved each other deeply. As we visited, I was introduced to a ritual that carried on between us for years. Whenever I arrived, Grace had a joke ready for me. She made me laugh and we proceeded in getting each other up to date with all that was going on in our lives. After visiting, I presented a hymn before serving them Holy Communion.

Along the way, I became fully aware of their daily routine. Whenever I think of it, I am reminded that it is easy to say the word *love*, but it is another thing to live it out. Every single day, Henry got Grace out of bed and into her wheelchair. Once in her chair, he took her to their bathroom to bathe and dress her. It was then off to the dining room. Henry had always been a hard worker, but he had now become a good cook. Once the meal was prepared, he sat down to feed his beloved wife. When done, he moved Grace to her favorite chair in the living room, where Grace had mastered the ability to place a pencil in her mouth and write detailed messages on a notepad. She could also take that pencil and dial her phone and activate the speaker. Henry had also installed a motorized lift on their van, and Grace loved to go out and see the sights.

It sounds like a cliché, but in the case of the Petersons, it's true: they never complained. A part of me was always waiting for the day when they might, but that day never came. I felt as though I had met two Christians who quite simply knew how to walk by faith and not by sight. They were happier than most couples I've met who otherwise seemed completely healthy.

All of this, however, doesn't make sense. Most people would judge that the Petersons should have lived in sadness and that those who are *healthy* should live in happiness. Not the case here. The Lord had intervened, and through the theology of the cross, this couple looked past the hardship and instead celebrated a marriage made in heaven.

This is the lens of faith. It is the balance of what is seen and unseen. This faith learns never to judge a book by its cover. When something happens or is happening in which we only see despair, we must return to faith. The Lord has promised to work good through all things—not *some* things, not even *most* things, but through *all* things (Romans 8:28); and if God is for us, who can be against us (Romans 8:31)? With these assurances, the Lord promises to work good no matter what we face, in every situation, no matter how dire it seems.

GOD IS ALWAYS GOOD
AND ANSWERS PRAYER FOR GOOD

Another one of those homebound members is a faithful pastor only a hundred years young. He has taught me many lessons. One of them came in a conversation we were having when I said in response to a pleasant report, "God is good." The wise old pastor said to me, "God is good whether this had happened or not."[16] He was right. There was no arguing his point. The child of God gets into an accident. If the person dies, God is good in taking His child into glory. If the individual survives with great hardship, he or she might grow in faith in ways never imagined. If the person survives and is granted healing, God is still good. The Lord knows what He is doing in

---

16   Herb Geisler, communion visitation in Lake Forest, California, ca. 2011–17.

any scenario, regardless of how we might struggle with it. A wise seminary professor once taught me and my classmates about prayer. He said, "There are three things to know about prayer:

1.   God always answers the prayers of His children.

2.   God always answers for good.

3.   God rarely answers the way we expect Him to."[17]

These are the things regarding what is seen and unseen. Here, the lens of faith comes into play. When we see something that makes us suspect that God is far away, faith reminds us that He is always close. Why does the Lord even do this? He is teaching us to walk by faith and not by sight. Besides, the things of sight get too easily entangled with the things of the world. What the world sees and considers impressive are oftentimes the very things that drag us away from God.

We should therefore not be surprised. What is unseen, those things that do not seem to be good, are often the very things used by God to keep us close to Him. In this way, there is a great reversal that comes into focus: those who are brought low are lifted up; but those who lift themselves up are brought low. This is not an appealing principle. The world does not see it this way. Who in their right mind wants to be brought low? Yet, this is exactly how God works. The lens of faith sees this, being able to see through what is otherwise undesirable, and yet countless Christians will testify that God conducted His greatest work in their lives when they went through great hardships.

Jesus was brought lower than anyone when the sins of the world were upon Him, but after that, He became higher than anyone, having won salvation for all. He did this when,

---

17   Robert Preus, lecture on "Justification" at Concordia Theological Seminary, Fort Wayne, Indiana, 1991.

as the innocent one, He became guilty so that the guilty (all humanity) would become innocent (this, by the way, is the true *great reversal*). Though once despised by people, He is Savior of all. His people reflect Him. His Christian-disciple-priests are brought low in His image so that they may also be lifted up. They learn to see that their crosses are not bad but good. Whatever keeps them hungry and thirsty for the grace of God must be treated as a great blessing. Whatever causes them to cry out is that which God uses to keep His people reliant upon Jesus Christ. This is the way of God:

> He also told this parable to some who trusted in themselves that they were righteous, and treated others with contempt: "Two men went up into the temple to pray, one a Pharisee and the other a tax collector. The Pharisee, standing by himself, prayed thus: 'God, I thank you that I am not like other men, extortioners, unjust, adulterers, or even like this tax collector. I fast twice a week; I give tithes of all that I get.' But the tax collector, standing far off, would not even lift up his eyes to heaven, but beat his breast, saying, 'God, be merciful to me, a sinner!' I tell you, this man went down to his house justified, rather than the other. For everyone who exalts himself will be humbled, but the one who humbles himself will be exalted." (Luke 18:9–14)

THE LUTHERAN LENS—WHAT IS REAL?

UNCOVER INFORMATION

1. Summarize the first three sets of lenses put forth in the first five chapters in your own words.

2. What are the two major parts, or aspects, of being human?

3. According to 2 Corinthians 5:7, how does the Christian "walk," or live?

4. What do we mean by the terms *theology of glory* and *theology of the cross*?

5. In what way is God hidden in Christ? in the Sacraments? in Christians?

DISCOVER MEANING

1. Describe how the right-side lenses of Christian-disciple-priest counter the left-side lenses of world-devil-sin.

2. When Ephesians 6:12 describes "heavenly places," to what is it basically referring?

3. If one is indeed walking by faith, what does this look like?

4. Why does God hide Himself?

5. The account of Naaman is presented in 2 Kings 5. Why was Naaman offended before he finally washed in the Jordan?

EXPLORE IMPLICATIONS

1. Given the importance of affirming one's identity as Christian-disciple-priest, what daily disciplines in thought, word, and deed might affirm identity in Christ?

2. If there is truly a spiritual *and* a physical reality (and there is), how should this reality impact the way we live?

3. It is easy to become discouraged by what we physically see. How does remembering the spiritual reality help in these moments of discouragement?

4. In respect to Romans 8:28, how should we see times of hardship?

5. Why do you think many Christians testify to growing in their faith through times of suffering and crisis?

CHAPTER 7

THE LUTHERAN LENS— WHAT AM I?

What is the Christian? The Christian is a sinner and one who has also been forgiven his or her sin. Christians are at the same time sinners and justified in Christ. It is important, however, that it is not forgotten what follows the status of having been justified. The justified one who is in Christ has also been given the Holy Spirit. So what is the Christian? Yes, he or she is a sinner, but the Christian is also one who has the Holy Spirit.

A CONFLICT, BUT NOT A STANDOFF

This sets up an important situation to understand in the life of faith. The first thing to know is that to be both a sinner and a forgiven child of God with the Holy Spirit means that the Christian must—necessarily—experience a conflict/struggle/battle that streams from the two realities. The second thing to understand is that these are not equal powers or forces. Sin is powerful, there is no question, and it causes a Christian to grieve. The Holy Spirit, however, leads us back to Jesus Christ and what He did about sin, and this causes a Christian to rejoice so that the grieving is overcome. "Weeping may tarry for the night, but joy comes with the morning" (Psalm 30:5). That means we cannot describe the Christian life as a standoff between two equal cosmic forces that leaves the Christian living with a devil on one shoulder and an angel on the other. Christ has defeated the devil, and the Christian knows Christ's victory, which has overcome the world (1 John 5:4).

While the Word of God clearly teaches about the conflict between the sin in us and the Holy Spirit in us, this does not mean that the Christian as an individual "I" is schizoid or in possession of a split personality.[18] Rather, the Christian within him- or herself experiences the opposing forces of what we discussed above: the world, the devil, and the sin that is within each person (on the one hand); and the Holy Spirit, the new creation or new status in Christ that He brings, along with the born-again spirit that lives by faith in Christ (on the other).

This is to say that the Christian is well familiar with the ongoing conflict between these opposing forces. It is critical, however, to embark on further consideration of this duality in the right way. Three major clarifications need to be made:

1. The conflict itself is not an indication that a Christian is not really a Christian. Much to the contrary, the conflict is a crucial sign that a Christian is truly a Christian.

2. The conflict, however, is not the Christian's focus, as if the conflict were a badge to take pride in or a suffering that *makes them* real Christians. Rather, its real purpose is to lead Christians back to Christ, their true focus.

3. The conflict is surpassed by an even more important experience, namely, the Christian's life in the Spirit—the daily remaining in Christ—which leads to living in faith and the active expression of that faith, especially love, which is the ongoing work of the Holy Spirit.

18   Michael P. Middendorf, *Romans 1–8*, Concordia Commentary (St. Louis: Concordia Publishing House, 2013), 561.

THE CONFLICT IS NORMAL AND NECESSARY

First of all, it is important to know that the Scriptures do not present the Christian conflict as something strange or abnormal. Too many Christians, however, have been given the impression that if they continue in conflict, then their faith must be lacking, or perhaps they are not Christians at all (or at the very least, not "Spirit-filled" or "mature"). False teachers present a triumphalism in the lives of Christians so that Christians are not supposed to continue to struggle against sin. Instead, false teaching asserts, true Christians advance beyond the struggle.

What happens in the light of such teaching? If Christians begin to believe this false presentation of God's Word but then inevitably continue to struggle with sin, then they are often filled with doubt about their status in Christ. They might question whether they are really children of God. Such false teaching can produce a misguided despair. If this happens, other problems develop, but the most serious problem is losing faith in Christ who came for sinners.

On the other hand, Christians might convince themselves that they are indeed advancing beyond the struggle against sin. They will deceive themselves into believing that they are, according to this false view, better than other Christians who still struggle. Such false teaching can produce prideful delusion. If this happens, other problems develop, but the most serious problem is losing reliance upon Christ and replacing the Gospel with perceived self-advancement. Such thinking leads to modern-day Pharisees who, like those at the time of Christ, consider themselves better than others.

One of the most influential leaders of popular American Christianity in the twentieth century and the first part of the twenty-first century proposed stages of Christian development within the Christian life. Inherent in this teaching is the notion that as Christians advance, their struggle against sin also diminishes. This is a very dangerous idea. The popular teaching proposed five levels among Christians: (1) the humanized Christian, who may or may not actually be a Christian; (2) the carnal Christian/defeated Christian, who is a true Christian but still compromises by living sinfully; (3) the spirit-controlled/radiant Christian, who is not only forgiven but also obediently follows Christ; (4) the spiritually mature Christian, who has learned advanced self-control; and (5) the spiritual father, who leads others to conversion. This top-level Christian has learned complete surrender to God when carrying out God's perfect will according to a unique understanding of Romans 12:2.[19]

These approaches to the ongoing conflict, however, ignore the fact that the Word of Christ teaches that the spiritual battle in the life of the Christian is real. As a matter of fact, the more Christians grow in their faith, the more aware they become of their sin and the more they react to it by returning to Jesus Christ. That is, while it is true that Christians may in fact grow and mature in their faith, it is not true that this is apparent through a diminishing struggle. The exact opposite is true; the struggle can even seem to intensify. Luther provides this insight:

> When you have wicked thoughts, you should not on this account despair; only be on your guard lest you be taken captive by them. . . . Wherever faith comes into being, there come a hundred evil thoughts and a hundred temptations more than before. Only see to it that you act the man; do not suffer yourself to be taken captive; continue to resist and to say: I will not, I will not.[20]

---

19   Alfonso Odilon Espinosa, "The Apocalyptic Anxiety of American Evangelicalism As Seen through *Left Behind* and Tim LaHaye's Programme for the Preservation of Evangelical Identity" (PhD dissertation, University of Birmingham, England, 2009), 232–33.

20   Francis Pieper, *Christian Dogmatics I* (St. Louis: Concordia Publishing House,

Ironically, if this conflict were to cease, then this would be the sign not of faith's advancement but of the loss of faith. As one theologian notes: "When in the lives of erstwhile believers the struggle of the spirit against the flesh has ceased and the sins have again become dominant, then these believers have fallen from faith."[21] If, however, Christians are concerned that their sins are dominating them, then this very concern is a sign that the battle continues. Unbelievers just don't care, because after all, they will reason, they are only human. The crisis of conscience, however, is indication that God has kept the Christian in the battle. To be in the struggle against sin itself means that the Christian does not desire to go along with sin. In response, the Christian runs again to Jesus Christ. This is what Christians do.

As for the battle, the Scriptures are as clear as day about its reality in the life of the Christian. Two main sections in the New Testament clearly describe the conflict and battle. The first is from Romans 7–8, while the second is from Galatians 5. Here is a key section on the battle from Romans 7 (Romans 8 will be considered further below):

> For I know that nothing good dwells in me, that is, in my flesh. For I have the desire to do what is right, but not the ability to carry it out. For I do not do the good I want, but the evil I do not want is what I keep on doing. Now if I do what I do not want, it is no longer I who do it, but sin that dwells within me. So I find it to be a law that when I want to do right, evil lies close at hand. For I delight in the law of God, in my inner being, but I see in my members another law waging war against the law of my mind and making me captive to the law of sin that dwells in my members. (Romans 7:18–23)

1950), 565.

21 Pieper, *Christian Dogmatics I*, 569.

FOUR FORCES IN THE BATTLE

One Lutheran theologian pointed out, "There are four forces" in the battle that the Christian experiences. They include "the Law of God, the other law, the law of the mind, [and] the law of sin in the members [Romans 7:22–23]."[22] *The Law of God* is the Law in the Word of God. As the Scriptures themselves teach, this Law is "holy and righteous and good" (Romans 7:12). There is, however, *the other law*, which is the power of sin in the world, which tries to overcome our lives with sin. *The law of the mind* is the Christian conscience that actively agrees with God's Law and desires and wills to be in conformity with the way of God, but *the law of sin in the members* is that quality of the sinful nature that desires to agree with the power of sin in the world. It is this quality (this fourth law), however, that has also been crucified with Christ and drowned in the waters of Holy Baptism. *The other law* tries to dig up our old, buried, sinful corpse. It tries to cause us to return to the old life that has died.

The battle lines are drawn up in a battle of two against two in the life of every Christian: the Law of God's Word and the law of the mind of the Christian agreeing with it versus the law of the power of sin partnered with the law of sin that dwells in human flesh. The battle is a serious one and very real. It is also painful and can seem agonizing to the Christian. This is the reason St. Paul cried out, "Wretched man that I am! Who will deliver me from this body of death? Thanks be to God through Jesus Christ our Lord!" (Romans 7:24–25).

St. Paul is here guiding Christians to the rest of the story, which is applicable to every Christian. He is being drawn by the Holy Spirit to the only Savior, the Lord Jesus Christ. This introduces an entirely different law altogether, namely "the law of

---

22   Martin H. Franzmann, *Romans: A Commentary* (St. Louis: Concordia Publishing House, 1968), 132.

the Spirit of life." Our consideration continues on to Romans 8:

> For the law of the Spirit of life has set you free in Christ
> Jesus from the law of sin and death. For God has done
> what the law, weakened by the flesh, could not do. By
> sending His own Son in the likeness of sinful flesh and
> for sin, He condemned sin in the flesh, in order that the
> righteous requirement of the law might be fulfilled in
> us, who walk not according to the flesh but according
> to the Spirit. (Romans 8:3–4)

The difference here is that the Holy Spirit does not permit a stalemate in the battle experienced by the Christian but instead secures a decisive victory. It is no longer two laws against two laws, but instead *three* laws against two laws where the Holy Spirit leads the Christian to win out. The Holy Spirit leads the Christian back to what Christ has accomplished for the sake of all people. The Holy Spirit leads us back to our lives in Christ, the one who fulfilled the Law in His life lived for all and who took upon Himself the condemnation of the Law in His death on the cross of Calvary. Furthermore, the Spirit leads Christians back to Christ, who has decisively conquered the power of sin and death through His glorious resurrection for all. If not for the reality of the conflict/struggle/battle, however, we would never see through the lens of faith our need for the Spirit's sanctifying work.

The second section on the Christian's constant battle is in Galatians 5:

> But I say, walk by the Spirit, and you will not gratify
> the desires of the flesh. For the desires of the flesh
> are against the Spirit, and the desires of the Spirit are
> against the flesh, for these are opposed to each other,
> to keep you from doing the things you want to do. But
> if you are led by the Spirit, you are not under the law.
> (Galatians 5:16–18)

NOT PREOCCUPIED WITH THE CONFLICT

This leads us to address the second consideration, that the conflict itself is not to be the Christian's focus. We mention this due to one of the most popular misinterpretations of Galatians 5. Too often, Galatians 5 is viewed as going both ways, namely, sometimes Christians are kept "from doing the things [they] want" with respect to the Spirit, and other times the Christians are kept "from doing the things [they] want" with respect to the flesh. This perspective implies two equally powerful entities. Such a view, however, gives too much credit to the flesh and not enough credit to the Spirit of God. The following commentary is particularly helpful in explaining why we should not go along with this compromising view:

> This interpretation should be rejected, since [Galatians] 5:17 so understood would hardly provide a supporting reason for 5:16's affirmation that walking by the Spirit will defeat the desire of the flesh. Why bother to walk by the Spirit if the flesh will nevertheless defeat the Spirit? The Spirit would not be an effective counter to the flesh. The Spirit would be no more effective than Moses' Law. Paul never entertains a stalemate in the battle against the flesh.[23]

These words also imply that we should have a proper understanding of *flesh*. Scripture uses the word in different ways. One use is to treat it as a representative of man's inability compared with what only God can do (e.g., Matthew 16:17). Another use is the physical body, as when St. Paul says that he received a "thorn . . . in [his] flesh" (2 Corinthians 12:7). There are other nuances beyond these as well. When St. Paul, however, puts the word *flesh* alongside "the Spirit," as when he contrasts the flesh with the Spirit of God, the word *flesh* is something contrary to the Holy Spirit.

23   Andrew A. Das, *Galatians,* Concordia Commentary (St. Louis: Concordia Publishing House, 2014), 563–64.

Flesh in this latter way is how the word is used in Galatians 5. In this context, *flesh* is abstract and not a natural quality of what it means to be human. It is not a part of created person-hood. Instead, the idea is "a power at work in the universe."[24] This power works upon people in a similar manner as what was described above in "the other law" in Romans 7, which refers to the power of sin in the world.

However, once the Holy Spirit leads the Christian to no longer be dominated by this power, or "other law," the conflict/struggle/battle should no longer be considered hopeless; the Word of God will not legitimize that sort of pessimism. St. John wrote, "The reason the Son of God appeared was to destroy the works of the devil" (1 John 3:8). When the Christian does not recognize Christ's victory, then sin is put on a pedestal. Sin is glorified and again, the flesh gets too much credit. As one theologian explains, "Dwelling on personal sins becomes its own form of idolatry!"[25] The Christian has no excuse to wallow in self-pity because of the conflict. The same theologian points out, "[Paul] will broach no idolatrous self-absorption with the 'miserable' struggle. This is an exercise in vanity."[26] It is also an exercise that can reject the Gospel, believing that the sin and its resultant struggle are too overwhelming, even for the Gospel of Christ. The struggle, however, is only intended to lead the Christian back to Christ alone.

THE CHRISTIAN'S FOCUS: GETTING BACK TO CHRIST EVERY SINGLE DAY

The third and last consideration is that the Christian should understand the resultant life that follows liberation from the power of sin. This is the new experience that should not be ne-glected or downplayed in the life of the Church. Galatians 5:24

24   Das, *Galatians,* 594.
25   Das, *Galatians,* 589.
26   Das, *Galatians,* 594.

says, "And those who belong to Christ Jesus have crucified the flesh with its passions and desires." It is true that the Christian is the active agent here in Galatians 5, but the context of Scripture qualifies our understanding of what this means. Contextually, other passages in Galatians teach that the Christian has been *passively* crucified with Christ (Galatians 2:19–20; 6:14).[27] The scriptural emphasis is that being crucified with Christ is God's action upon the Christian. It is something *He* does to the Christian and for the Christian. The passive emphasis should be maintained. Galatians 2:19–20 and 6:14 provide a framing understanding for Galatians 5. Here are those other verses:

> For through the law I died to the law, so that I might live to God. I have been crucified with Christ. It is no longer I who live, but Christ who lives in me. And the life I now live in the flesh I live by faith in the Son of God, who loved me and gave Himself for me. (Galatians 2:19–20)

> But far be it from me to boast except in the cross of our Lord Jesus Christ, by which the world has been crucified to me, and I to the world. (Galatians 6:14)

Losing this understanding of the Christian being freed from the domination of sin by being (passively) crucified with Christ automatically means the Christian life (so imagined) will only be a return to the Law and man's effort. Such an approach is doomed to fail. If this happens, then the so-called "Christian life" will be an exercise in futility. The believer must be fully convinced of what God has *already done* for him or her:

> [Galatians] 2:19–20 provides the foundation for 5:24 by explaining that the crucified Christ now lives in the believer. The believer lives as the crucified Christ. Gal 5:24 is best understood as expressing the indicative of

---

27   Das, *Galatians*, 586.

what the believer decisively *did* in Christ. The believer, who *crucified* the flesh, *is* holy. **The death of the flesh is a past event**. The flesh belongs to the old order that is passing away. The Christian is no longer a slave of sin (2:17) since **the decisive victory** that took place at Christ's cross is **also a decisive victory** that took place in the life of the believer (cf. also Baptism in 3:27–28).[28]

The "decisive victory" is *both* Calvary's cross *and* the new life of the Holy Spirit, who keeps us in Christ. In this life of Christ, faith is active. It knows what was described by Chemnitz in chapter 3 in his last point, defining faith that includes "a confidence . . . which has access to God . . . [and] 'the joy of the Spirit,' . . . so that the heart, feeling the new life and joy in God, happily rests in the promise of grace, even under the cross."[29] This new life, however, does not merely translate into a blessed conscience for the Christian; it also leads to good works that God has prepared in advance for Christians to do (Ephesians 2:10). Luther's description of faith is also a description of life in the Spirit:

> Faith, however, is a divine work in us which changes us and makes us to be born anew of God, John 1[:12–13]. It kills the old Adam and makes us altogether different men, in heart and spirit and mind and powers; and brings with it the Holy Spirit. O it is a living, busy, active, mighty thing, this faith. It is impossible for it not to be doing good works incessantly. It does not ask whether good works are to be done, but before the question is asked, it has already done them, and is constantly doing them. Whoever does not do such works, however, is an unbeliever.[30]

The lens of faith regarding what the Christian is helps

---

28   Das, *Galatians,* 586–87, emphasis added.
29   Chemnitz, *Loci,* 502.
30   AE 35:370.

Christians to live out their faith more confidently. The conflict Christians experience does not mean they are abnormal. Jesus only invites those who "labor [are weary] and [are] heavy laden" (Matthew 11:28). The Apology of the Augsburg Confession in the Lutheran Confessions explains, "The 'labor' and the burden signify the contrition, anxiety, and terrors of sin and death."[31] Again, this is part of the normal Christian life.

Still, the Christian is not to become transfixed on the struggle. It serves a purpose and is not intended by God for any kind of preoccupation with the struggle itself. When the battle is misconstrued, it is easy to enter extremes of either living in despair (believing that our sinful struggle is too powerful for the Gospel of Christ) or delusion (believing that through the struggle itself, we earn the right to be identified as Christians). Instead, the conflict is to lead us to Jesus Christ, who is the only answer to the power of sin. When the Holy Spirit leads us to Christ, then we are redirected to what Christ has already accomplished (past tense) in winning the victory over the power of sin. Since we are joined to Christ in Holy Baptism, we share in His victory. Just as we enter Christ's death and burial through Baptism, we are also joined to Him—the resurrected Lord—for "newness of life" (Romans 6:3–4).

That is, two things fundamentally mark the Christian life: a painful conflict (on account of the Christian's confrontation with the power of sin) and the new life of the Spirit (on account of the Christian being joined to Jesus Christ, who conquered the power of sin). Conflict on the one hand, and new life on the other—this is the lens that describes what Christians experience.

Gerald, who is now in heaven, seemed happy for my home visit. I was the new pastor and he took me seriously when I extended an invitation to the congregation to share with me

---

31   Ap XIIA (V) 44.

how I might especially and personally serve the members of the church in addition to the regular service of Word and Sacrament. I stated my desire to come to my parishioners privately through home visits or meeting them at the church in my study. Gerald took me up on the offer.

He wanted me to know about his long battle with alcohol. As a result of this struggle in his life, he thought it important that his new pastor be aware about the ongoing threat. "Pastor, if I have even the slightest bit of alcohol, I will relapse and lose all self-control. Please pray for my protection. Keep an eye on me and please be aware that this is a real concern in my life." As Gerald was relating his very real struggle with me, my mind immediately started to anticipate where this conversation would go in respect to the Sacrament of the Altar. Gerald was most likely going to apply his concerns regarding the alcohol in the Communion wine.

Gerald kept elaborating on his struggle. He had come a long way and had developed a protective hedge in his life. His extended family was aware, as were his closest friends, and now I was aware. He was serious and wise to have enlisted such a strong support group. I was impressed by his humility and his understanding of the Holy Church, the mutual love and bearing of one another's burdens practiced in the Body of Christ. Still, I was getting a little anxious about what might be discussed regarding the Supper. Sometimes people had funny ideas.

I couldn't take it any further. We had been talking about his struggle for at least an hour and he hadn't broached the Sacrament. I had already formulated what I thought I should say: "Gerald, I just want you to know that you have nothing to worry about regarding Holy Communion. We will be offering a nonalcoholic option that is still wine but with a much lower alcohol content. If necessary, I will even consider intinction, and if you're still concerned, we could start a regular and frequent practice of individual Confession and Absolution." While I was going through my brainstorm of possible solutions, Gerald had a perplexed and almost pained look on his face. I just didn't know why he was reacting as he was.

When I finished, feeling I should wrap up my recommended approach sooner than later, he jumped in: "Pastor, thank you, but I am not at all concerned about the wine in the Holy Sacrament." He seemed almost a little embarrassed, not for himself but for me. "The Lord would never allow me to be harmed through His holy blood."

I am not writing a prescription for what should be the attitude and practice of all Christians regarding alcoholism and the Sacrament, not at all; but I am writing a description of this Christian's experience. His struggle was yet another manifestation of the spiritual battle. He felt the power of sin. He felt the sinful allurement to be mastered by alcohol and to lose all restraint. What he had experienced in his past was misery through the domination by alcohol. The prospect of returning to this state raised fear and trembling in his heart. Gerald was well familiar with the conflict/struggle/battle.

At the same time, Gerald was not overwhelmed by the conflict. He knew the Spirit's guidance, comfort, and power in Christ. The first sign of this was his liberation that enabled him to reach out to me and invite me to his home. The second sign of his new life was his ability to confess his struggle and constructively discuss it with his pastor. The third sign of his life in the Spirit over and above the conflict itself was his utter clarity regarding his comfort and confidence for receiving the Holy Sacrament of the Lord's body and blood. While he feared the prospect of returning to his old life, he nevertheless was not dominated by that fear. God's perfect love had driven out Gerald's fear (1 John 4:18). He was now living in the freedom of the Spirit. He was firmly rooted in Christ, and He yearned for the blood of the Lamb without any concern that it could possibly cause him any harm.

It was one of those instances when I was blown away by the testimony of one of my flock. It was one of those visitations that was a greater blessing *for* the pastor than any blessing brought *by* the pastor. I got a glimpse of the work of the Holy Spirit. I got a glimpse of what a Christian is. Gerald was testimony to the lens of faith that sees clearly: we are supposed to be in a conflict, and we are supposed to know the life of the Spirit of God, who keeps us in Christ.

CHAPTER 7
DISCUSSION GUIDE:

THE LUTHERAN LENS—WHAT AM I?

UNCOVER INFORMATION

1. In the context of this chapter, what is a Christian?

2. What is the problem with the idea that if one struggles less, then this must mean that one has a stronger faith and is more holy?

3. List "the four forces in the battle" (save the fifth law for now). Which ones are good and which ones are bad?

4. What is meant by "Don't become preoccupied with the conflict"?

5. What is the decisive victory given to the Christian?

DISCOVER MEANING

1. Why is the conflict/struggle/battle a necessary experience in the Christian life?

2. How can a false view of the conflict lead to either despair or delusion?

3. Describe the *other law* in your own words.

4. Regarding the conflict as described in Galatians 5, what is meant by *flesh*?

5. How does Chemnitz describe faith? How does Luther describe faith?

EXPLORE IMPLICATIONS

1. If a Christian does not fully realize that the conflict is normal and necessary, what unnecessary problems might develop in the Christian's mind?

2. Luther associates faith with increasing awareness of sin and temptation. Why should this be so?

3. A fifth law is introduced in Romans 8. What is it, and what difference does it make in the life of the Christian?

4. What has God done for and to the Christian against the threat of the flesh? What are the implications for the Christian life now that this has been done?

5. What two things fundamentally mark the Christian life? Why is it so important to know this?

CHAPTER 8

THE LUTHERAN LENS— TO WHOM AM I SPEAKING?

It is one thing to grasp a situation through insight of what is seen and unseen, and furthermore, to have a good handle on oneself as a Christian—as one in spiritual conflict, but also with life in the Spirit. It is yet another thing to know the person in front of you. This chapter will consider not one more lens of faith (one more duality), but two more lenses (two more dualities). These are needed to properly view whomever we are speaking to.

FIRST *TO WHOM* LENS: THE INCLUSIVE AND EXCLUSIVE GOSPEL

The first lens is true for whomever we are interacting with: that person is someone God wants to be saved (as they are objectively already saved; but subjectively, they may not yet have faith to appropriate the objective salvation). This requires the lens of faith that knows this Gospel to be both and at the same time *inclusive* and *exclusive*. This is the lens of faith we will speak of first in this chapter. Those to whom we speak are called to know that they are offered an *inclusive* Gospel, and at the same time, they are called to know and confess the *exclusive* Savior.

SECOND *TO WHOM* LENS: DOES THE PERSON KNOW HIS OR HER NEED AND HELPLESSNESS, OR NOT?

The second lens is for knowing how to apply the inclusive and exclusive Gospel to a unique individual. Here, we need to know where a person is in respect to faith in Jesus Christ. We are not here to invest in labels. We are only trying to understand how to best apply God's love to a given person. Labels are often misused, and furthermore, they are often inaccurate. We want this second lens of faith to be easy: we should know whether those to whom we speak feel they need the Gospel while being convinced that there is nothing they can do to save themselves. This is, therefore, the second lens of faith: feeling the need and knowing one's personal inability, or not. That's it. Regardless of where people are, they are loved by God and forgiven their sins. At the same time, the Christian should only share the Gospel if the one to whom they speak is ready for it. This is the second lens discussed in this chapter.

THE AMAZING, ALL-INCLUSIVE LOVE OF GOD

Let us now consider the first lens: the people we are spending time with—regardless of who or what they are—are absolutely, positively loved by God. We must be clear about the singular framework for the Christian's engagement with *any* person, namely, love. This is always the first step toward another. Love is the light behind this lens of faith.

Love should always drive the interaction between the Christian and whomever they are interacting with. Any special consideration or adjustment, such as when to share Law or Gospel, will simply be an application of this same driving love. The second lens therefore becomes a matter of love's application. Before we get too far ahead of ourselves, though, what is love, and from where does it come?

As is well-known, the word *love* has more than one meaning, among them "affection" and "desire," but for our consideration, we are especially interested in the meaning as it's used in what is perhaps the most widely known Scripture verse: John 3:16. That verse says, "For God so loved the world, that He gave His only Son, that whoever believes in Him should not perish but have eternal life." *Love* in this sense is sacrificial. It expresses a commitment so profound that the lover is willing to give indescribably for the sake of the beloved. It is loving the other more than oneself. This is the love that God had and has toward us.

Driven by this love, God gave up His Son, Jesus Christ, for you and all other people. This love is so much *of* God that in 1 John 4, verses 8 and 16 reveal that "God is love." God is the one whose very nature is to extend Himself—sacrificially—for the good of the beloved. The amazing part of this is that the "beloved" through Jesus Christ is everyone. This is not an exaggeration: *everyone*.

This love, therefore, is not at all common. It is uncommon. Why? Because from a human perspective, if one is to give so much to another, then that person should be worthy of such love. This is the difference between God and people. Our love—apart from God in our lives—insists that the beloved deserve our love, that the beloved be worthy of our love. God's love insists on loving those who do not and are not.

St. Paul gives a detailed description of God's uncanny love:

> For while we were still weak, at the right time Christ died for the ungodly. . . . But God shows His love for us in that while we were still sinners, Christ died for us. . . . For if while we were enemies we were reconciled to God by the death of His Son, much more, now that we are reconciled, shall we be saved by His life. (Romans 5:6, 8, 10)

The objects of God's love—all of us—are described in ways that typically would not make anyone very endearing or attractive. God loved us sacrificially through the death of His Son while those for whom He died—all people—were weak, ungodly, sinners, and enemies of God. What was there to make us worthy of the love of God? Not only does God know humanity as helpless sinners who violate His Holy Law, but also as people who fought and still fight against Him. Would anyone else ever love such people? God is the only one, through Jesus Christ, who does.

This is how much God loves you. This is how much God loves all people.

UNIVERSAL GRACE

We should never underestimate what this says about the Christian faith. The faith of Christ is inclusive, fantastically inclusive, and it has been proven in real history. The pivotal teaching of the Christian faith is that the life, death, and resurrection of Jesus Christ rescues all people from sin, death, and the power of the devil. What Christ did in these was win forgiveness of sins, life, and salvation for all people. This is an objective fact. These gifts of salvation have been accomplished for every single person who has ever lived, is living, and ever will live. This is what the Church refers to as *universal grace*. This is what makes the Christian faith wonderfully inclusive.

The Christian faith permits anyone to be informed of this fact: God loves them in Christ and has already backed up His love through what Jesus Christ has already done for them. God has forgiven them (accomplished fact) and therefore loves and forgives them today. Again, this is completed action, and it was especially punctuated when the Lord Jesus Christ was dying on the cross and He said, "It is finished" (John 19:30). All that was required to pay the ransom for the redemption of all people for all time was finished. It was completed. Salvation is done, and God's love is now guaranteed.

Based on this state of affairs, God's love is unconditional even in the face of any personal circumstances and details in the lives of people today. It is unconditional precisely because it is already accomplished. God loves your neighbor across the street, your co-worker, your classmates, your relatives, and everyone else in your life. This is certain. There is no doubt about it. Salvation has been won for each and every one.

Some people get nervous about this teaching and inherently challenge the universal grace of God (where *grace* means "God's undeserved love and mercy in Christ"): "But doesn't a person 'have' to have faith in order to be saved?" The answer is, "Yes, of course," but this is the part that many people don't understand. It is this very characteristic of the inclusive, accomplished Gospel that makes it so powerful. When the Gospel is proclaimed, those who hear it are already assured that their forgiveness and salvation are firm. Faith in this Gospel does not make the Gospel effective; rather, the Gospel gives faith and makes faith effective. The Gospel—by the Holy Spirit who works through it—leads a person to grasp its inclusive guarantee. The person who hears it has the chance to see what makes the Gospel so wonderful: *It is for me and has already been done for me!*

GOD'S UNCONDITIONAL LOVE
AND MERCY MAKE GRACE UNIVERSAL

Will everyone therefore necessarily come to saving faith? No, but this does not cancel the power of the accomplished Gospel for all people. The Gospel's universal application is secure, and it is this guarantee that the Spirit of God uses to draw people who once assumed they had to do something first or be something first in order to be qualified for salvation. In the split second that someone hears the Gospel and realizes that no one is excluded from God's love in Jesus Christ whether faith already exists in them or not, then that person encounters an overwhelming love: *God loves me so much that He doesn't wait for my response to love Him back, but He loves me anyway*. God's unconditional love is effective even before anyone believes it.

This can seem like a mind bender, but it doesn't have to be. The story is told of a benevolent billionaire who decided to gift a classroom of university students with unexpected grants of $100,000 each. He personally came to the chosen class to announce his prearranged deposit into their personal bank accounts (even as it remained a mystery as to how he accessed their personal accounts). His gift was solid. It was objectively factual. What followed his coming into the classroom with what some might construe as a crazy announcement, however, provoked a divided response among the students.

Some of the students were utterly incredulous: "This is ridiculous, and there is no way anyone could or would do such a thing." These students considered the man's visit to be a prank, and they wondered if someone was secretly taping their class for a psych experiment. As a result of their unbelief, the incredulous students never accessed their financial gift. They went on living as if the money didn't exist. Consequently, they never used the money and therefore never enjoyed its benefits. Their unbelief, however, did not cancel the gift. Living their lives without knowing the benefits did not cause the gift to vanish. It was always theirs, but they never got anything out of it. Those students who did believe the benefactor, however, made immediate withdrawals and investments. The believing ones benefited from the gift.

This hypothetical illustration might not satisfy some who

need to stay closer to real life. It is challenging to put so much on any human being as representing unconditional love, but there are many people who will testify to having known someone like this. Maybe a grandparent, a friend, or a teacher once demonstrated this kind of love. I got to see it in my mother. She had her problems like any other person, but she was always there for me, even when I was a pain. She always had my back. I don't have to look far for a real-life example of unconditional love, but I also saw it in other people besides my beloved mother.

John was a spiritual mentor to me and was also the man who hired me for my first real job. In high school, I worked summers for him and his family-owned business. They were farmers and at the time, they had a very active and busy farm producing grapes, raisins, and cotton. Over the years, John gradually allowed me to take on more and more responsibilities. One summer, I had earned the privilege of starting basic tractor operations.

In the hot valley, a lot of dust was raised on and around the grapevines. This was a problem not only for the produce but also for the workers who would later access the vines. My job was to run a water tank hitched to my tractor, spraying water to reduce the accumulation of dust. I had to maintain the motor on the water tank so that the spray would be continuous, and when I drove out and back into the lanes of grapevines, it was best that I made my U-turns quickly and efficiently so as not to waste the water. I got pretty good at this, until one afternoon when I was a little careless and tried to make too sharp a U-turn.

My angle was too severe and I ended up pinching the hitch between the tractor and the water tank. I knew enough to take a deep breath and remind myself not to panic. It was now on me to maneuver the tractor to get out of the pinch, get realigned, and get back to my job. The only problem was that in my efforts to get out of my predicament, I not only did not make the situation better, but I made everything worse. I made it so much worse, in fact, that I was in jeopardy of breaking the hitch altogether. As my living nightmare continued, the water tank pitched sideways so that it was on the verge of tipping over. I had an incredible mess on my hands.

Right about this time, I started to think of the next potential problem: what if John saw what was going on? In my opinion, John was the epitome of a Christian man, but this was work, and I would assuredly be in deep trouble. He would certainly be angry, and my failure might cost me my job. I would not be able to blame him.

I couldn't save myself. And then, John saw me as he was driving by in his pickup. A feeling of dread came over me. It was a hot, miserable day. We were both sweating and tired, and now this catastrophe. I could not imagine how he was about to lay into me. I braced myself for the worst. John drove up and analyzed the situation while noting the condition of his farm equipment. He must have surely also noticed his employee's look of complete helplessness (and considerable embarrassment).

John didn't say a word. In fact, I don't even remember a grimace, furling eyebrows, agitated grunt, slight verbal complaint, or other angry expression. Nothing. He hopped up onto the tractor and in five or ten minutes, he got me out of my mess, got the tractor aligned to enter the next lane of vines, promptly got off, and handed everything back to me. I was not chastised. I was not blamed. I was not made the object of ridicule or judgment. He came, he saw, he helped, and he treated me like someone he still trusted. I was almost in a state of shock. I had never experienced anything like this in my entire life. When I saw him after that workday was over, he never brought it up. It was as if the whole thing had never happened. Even after all these years, after we became much closer and he became one of my most important supporters as I pursued the holy ministry, all I can think of is that this man loved me. To this day, from my standpoint, that love was completely unconditional.

The Gospel is like this but infinitely better. If a Christian were to ever give an unbeliever the impression that God somehow loved the Christian more, then it would be clear that the Christian, ironically, didn't understand the gift that saves him or her. There can be no claim that God loves some more than others. He doesn't. He loves all, and the sacrifice of His Son—as well as His Son's sacrifice of His very life's blood—establishes that God is positively for all people. Everyone gets the deposit of God's unconditional love into their personal spiritual bank account. Along the way, it is firmly established that the Gospel—and therefore the Christian faith—is 100 percent inclusive. God's eternal love is given to all, regardless of how hard we try to create messes in our lives. God just does not hold it against us. He gets us "realigned" and then treats us as if we had never sinned. This is how God loves everyone through Jesus Christ.

The Lutheran Confessions uphold this inclusive aspect of the Gospel: "Just as the preaching of repentance is universal, so also the promise of the Gospel is universal, that is, it belongs to all people."[32] It then goes on to offer these Scriptures to substantiate this confession:

> Repentance and forgiveness of sins should be proclaimed in His name to all nations. (Luke 24:47)

> For God so loved the world, that He gave His only Son. (John 3:16)

---

32   FC SD XI 28.

Behold, the Lamb of God, who takes away the sin of the world! (John 1:29)

The bread that I will give for the life of the world is My flesh. (John 6:51)

The blood of Jesus His Son cleanses us from all sin. (1 John 1:7)

[Jesus] is the propitiation for our sins, and not for ours only but also for the sins of the whole world. (1 John 2:2)

Come to Me, all who labor and are heavy laden, and I will give you rest. (Matthew 11:28)

For God has consigned all to disobedience, that He may have mercy on all. (Romans 11:32)

Not wishing that any should perish, but that all should reach repentance. (2 Peter 3:9)

The same Lord is Lord of all, bestowing His riches on all who call on Him. (Romans 10:12)

The righteousness of God through faith in Jesus Christ [is] for all who believe. (Romans 3:22)

For this is the will of My Father, that everyone who looks on the Son and believes in Him should have eternal life. (John 6:40)[33]

THE GOSPEL IS ALSO EXCLUSIVE

In today's culture, this point about the Gospel being totally inclusive cannot be emphasized enough. Ironically, many people included in God's unconditional love for them in Christ are offended by the Gospel because it is also exclusive. This is true: the Gospel is both inclusive and exclusive at the same time. When the Gospel's exclusivity becomes the focus, however, then it is often grounds for the Gospel to be considered offensive and untenable.

33   FC SD XI 28.

The most important reason for the Gospel's exclusivity is to reveal how God has empirically dealt with the sin that once separated God and man, and—as a result—makes God's inclusive love known in human history. Without its exclusivity, the Gospel would be neither possible nor knowable. Without its exclusivity, the Gospel would only be a theoretical. "God's love" would hang in the air as an ideal or an idea, but there would be nothing in human history capable of confirming God's inclusive, unconditional love. Without the Gospel's exclusivity, we would never know the Gospel's inclusivity.

God's inclusive love is known through the exclusive act of God sending His Son into human history, joining humanity as a fellow human, and empirically dealing with humanity's sin problem. This means that God's unconditional love is known and guaranteed through the real-history events of the life, death, and resurrection of the Lord Jesus Christ. Thus, if people want to know whether or not God really loves them, they can be directed through Christ's Word and Sacraments to the real-life event that proves God's love, namely, the saving service of the Lord Jesus Christ conducted for all people.

Jesus Himself taught—not in exclusive pride but in inclusive love—the necessary truth about God's unconditional love: "Jesus said to him, 'I am the way, and the truth, and the life. No one comes to the Father except through Me'" (John 14:6). Jesus reveals this to people who need to be saved from sin and death. It is similar to someone helping a man dying of thirst. In unconditional and inclusive love, they come offering water: "This water will save your life, and the only way that it will is if you take it and drink it." Imagine someone complaining at this juncture, "How offensive and closed-minded it is that I am now required to drink this water in order to save my life!" But the command to take and drink what saves is in itself part of the loving rescue and invitation to life. Jesus gives living water for eternal life (John 4:14). Saying Jesus is the only way to eternal life is like asserting that water is the fundamental element necessary for life on earth. These are seemingly grandiose claims, but both are true.

This exclusive claim, however, leads us back to why some people are offended. How can such a position be true in light of other religions and spiritualities? Such scrutiny generates the complaint that the Christian faith is basically disrespectful and narrow-minded. Because of this popular cultural complaint, many view Christians who claim to advocate unconditional love in theory as contradicting themselves in practice. The situation is enough to even tempt Christians to second-guess the exclusivity of the Gospel.

NOT CONTRADICTORY, BUT COMPLEMENTARY

This criticism against the Christian faith, however, should be reconsidered. Behind the objection is the assumption that it is impossible for faith to be both inclusive and exclusive at the same time. Is this a valid criticism? The answer is that such a paradox is neither logically nor theologically problematic. We are simply dealing with another lens of faith designed to show us what can be known, what is real, and what is true.

The world, however, likes the popular objection against Christianity's exclusivity because it has gone along with the cultural shift that no longer treats theology as objective truth about God and salvation. Instead, the culture has reclassified theology as "religion," and religion is no longer viewed as something that is objective. Instead, most would say that religion is subjective based on personal preferences and/or cultural practices. "After all," the culture says, "religion is based simply on what a person believes, so how can this in any way be objective, much less universal?" In other words, in the eyes of the world, religion is relative. Out of necessity, therefore, it must change and shift since it is based on nothing but ever-fluctuating personal preferences.

In this view, it is never appropriate to treat religious ideas as being objectively true for all people for all time. Instead, once again, religion depends on changing and shifting beliefs and rituals. In this view, only science is objective, but faith is not. If this dichotomy is true, then to claim religious exclusivism is just wrong.

There is no reason, however, to go along with the assumption that what is inclusive cannot be or should not be exclusive at the same time. It is not at all unreasonable to assert that the Christian faith is objectively true. There are many things in life that demonstrate the possibility of something being both inclusive and exclusive simultaneously. We will consider examples from the realm of science, the realm of human relationships, and cultural artifacts, and then look at the testimony of the Scriptures themselves.

COMPLEMENTARITY ACCORDING TO SCIENCE

Air and water are two resources that are inherently inclusive. That is, these are normally available to all people—universally—on planet earth. Now imagine someone complaining about this fact in the face of the molecular structure of air (O_2) and water (H_2O). What if a skeptic said, "The molecular structure of air and water is politically and culturally offensive. Other things and other molecular structures in this world should be treated as being just as essential as air and water for life's existence on planet earth. Air and water should never be considered the most important life-giving resources. Furthermore, air and water should be rejected as being essential"?

No one would ever go along with such opinions. Why not? Because the reality and essential nature of air and water is objectively verifiable. Yet, the fact is that air and water are inclusive, as these sustain the lives of all people; but they are also exclusive in that nothing else can remove their uniqueness and necessity. These facts are not at all offensive. In fact, to know this state of affairs—even if just intuitively—is to also benefit from air and water. Everyone knows that these resources are intended for all people and that their uniqueness sustains life itself. Who is going to complain about their inclusive and exclusive status?

COMPLEMENTARITY ACCORDING TO RELATIONSHIPS

This principle also enters the realm of human relationships. It is practically a universal human need and value to be close to another person. We are not, by the way, assuming any particular kind of relationship. The other person that is valued or needed may be family or a friend. People seem to know inherently that they are not meant to be alone. As this need is considered, we can also appreciate that the universal principle does not depend on any quality or attribute of a person's identity. People across the board have need for other human contact and relationship regardless of age, nationality, gender, or any other difference between human beings. It doesn't matter; the universal desire and need are there.

At the same time, once a particular person—a unique individual—is identified as fulfilling this longing for relationship, then the inclusive principle finds exclusive expression. In Scripture, not just anyone was King David's closest friend, but Jonathan was (1 Samuel 18:1). There was only one Jonathan like this in King David's life. If one is married—and while it is true that theoretically one might have married someone else—once that special person is identified as spouse, then that spouse fills that role exclusively. The principle of inclusivity is made manifest in an exclusive and unique relationship.

COMPLEMENTARITY ACCORDING
TO CULTURAL ARTIFACTS

This "both-and" reality is also known in many cultural artifacts. For example, philosophically, people can find athletic expression in many ways. There are many sports, many workouts, and many approaches to athletic exertion. If, however, one attended a major league baseball game but then all of a sudden noticed that the game between the Los Angeles Dodgers and New York Yankees didn't include nine regular innings but was reduced to only two innings on a given night, pandemonium would erupt. Who changed the rules? How can such a travesty count for a real baseball game? How soon will tickets be refunded? The universal nature of sports nevertheless finds exclusive and one-of-a-kind expression in baseball, including nine regular innings for every MLB game.

The examples of cultural artifacts are countless. We need food and want food, but it would be sheer confusion to go to a Chinese restaurant and expect to be handed a menu for Mexican food. Food is inclusive and universal, but it is *expressed* in different ways. In the meantime, no one tries to transform kung pao chicken into cheese enchiladas. Inclusive principles contain exclusive expressions and parameters. If we try to change the exclusive details, however, then we inherently deny legitimate ways in which things are part of what is also inclusive. For example, Mexican food is an exclusive example of universal, inclusive food, but if we eliminate Mexican food—heaven forbid—then Mexican food is no longer part of the inclusive realm of food, because it would no longer exist.

But why not just plug the variety of world religions into the analogy of sports and food and just say that all religions are equally legitimate and equally true? At this juncture, one must take into consideration the unique claims of anything considered exclusive. The analogy still holds when we realize that baseball will not permit itself to be just a synonym for hockey. Someone might sincerely believe and even assert that baseball and hockey are the same sport, but they would be sincerely wrong. We must, therefore, take a last step and consider the unique truth claims of any exclusive sample of an inclusive and universal principle.

For example, a married spouse is the only one who wears the ring representing a singular marriage. Water is the only thing with the molecular structure H_2O. And when it comes to the wide variety of religions, all of them make unique claims about themselves (even if they claim that they are not at all exclusive, because that in itself would be an exclusive claim). Now, it is possible that someone might make different claims about marriage or molecular structures. Someone might say that his wife is blonde when she is brunette (and get into trouble later), etc. That is, the claims themselves can be tested and in many cases—especially when it comes to faith claims—ought to be tested.

If someone comes along and says that an official basketball rim is eleven feet high (instead of its regulation ten feet), then I will object, not because I am being unloving but because the assertion is untrue and inaccurate. If someone starts to assert that my wife is of Italian descent (as great as that nationality is), then I do not do her or anyone else any favors if I go along with it and thus deny her German heritage. In other words, we should consider the exclusive claims and we should test them. We should never be so lazy as to ignore them. If we do, we might be doing so to our own peril, and the things of faith are about life themes infinitely more important than baseball or even Mexican food (though this may be hard for some to believe).

What if, however, two major faith expressions claim to be exclusively true and yet inherently contradict each other? Then there are only three logical options: claim A is true and claim B is false; or claim A is false and claim B is true; or both claims A and B are false. What cannot be true, if the two claims are mutually exclusive and contradictory at the same place and time, is that both claims are true. Again, this is a process we would apply to any claim in life. We do it all the time. If a person calls an insurance agent inquiring about rates for a car under an insurance plan but receives contradictory information—perhaps one quote in an email and another quote over the phone—then the logical assumption is not that both quotes are accurate, but rather that at least one of them is inaccurate. No one would assume that both quotes are correct.

Such basic scrutiny should especially be conducted regarding the truth claims of the Christian faith compared with the truth claims of other religions and spiritual approaches to life. This is not even to say that other religions do not contain *elements* of truth, but this is not the question at hand. The question is, which one can be counted on for salvation beyond death? Which one should *ultimately* be trusted?

In considering overall reliability, it is an understatement to say that the credentials of the Christian faith are impressive. The Holy Bible is about real people in real events in real time and space. The Old and New Testaments are marked by (1) internal evidence showing consistency within the Holy Bible (many who claim that there are contradictions are typically unaware of biblical nuances); (2) external evidence that demonstrates alignment between the Holy Bible and other records of human history and archaeology; and (3) bibliographical evidence highlighting the fact that modern translations of the Holy Bible come from consistent, extensive numbers of early copies. Truth is demonstrated by the historical signs of truth (when what is said aligns with a real and actual state of affairs): early sources and eyewitness testimony, the kind of characteristics that step away from blind assertions and enter into the testable arena of falsifiability. The claims of the Christian faith can be checked out objectively.

The details of that last paragraph are worthy of another book, but what might be just as compelling to consider is the quality of the claims made as a final result of the objective standards. This faith offers the inclusive and unconditional love we have discussed above. Point of fact: it is the only faith, religious, or spiritual option that gives everything to a person up front, no strings attached. Even the faith that is needed to personally benefit from what is given is itself given by God through the Gospel proclaimed. What other religious or spiritual system can legitimately make this claim? In fact, what the many other options have in common is that their offerings come with strings attached; something must first be done on the part of the person. No work, no benefits. If there is no effort, then whatever represents love, freedom, liberation, nirvana, release, enlightenment, salvation, or whatever must be withheld. The exact opposite is true about the Christian faith: before I can lift a finger, the love of God in Jesus Christ is already mine.

COMPLEMENTARITY ACCORDING TO JESUS

Let us, however, make the situation even easier to consider and ask this basic question (which was a question that Jesus Himself once asked): "But who do you say that I am?" (Matthew 16:15). There are only so many answers that can be given. The Gospel gives a specific answer: Jesus Christ is the only true Son of God, who died and rose for all so that the love of God would be poured out for all. The answer is to heed the call to trust in Him alone so that the forgiveness of sins and eternal life might be personally had. Jesus Christ is where inclusivity and exclusivity for the sake of eternal life converge.

This truth is especially seen in Holy Scripture.

In the Gospel of St. Matthew, chapter 1 records the genealogy of Jesus Christ. One of St. Matthew's goals was to demonstrate to his fellow Jews that Jesus is the true Messiah. His genealogy traced Jesus' royal line and the patriarchs who had received God's promise about the future Savior. Embedded in this genealogy, however, is St. Matthew's inclusion of certain women. Their inclusion is startling and must have been shocking to some of the original receptors of what St. Matthew wrote.

St. Matthew included the following women in the genealogy of his Gospel's first chapter: Tamar (Matthew 1:3), Rahab (v. 5), Ruth (v. 5), and "the wife of Uriah," clearly referring to Bathsheba (v. 6). All four of these women would have been easily categorized as sinners by many Jews. They would have had good reason to assert this about these women. Tamar disguised herself as a prostitute and deceived her father-in-law into sleeping with her so that she could have a child to carry on the name of her dead husband (Genesis 38). Rahab was in fact a prostitute in Jericho who helped Israel's spies (Joshua 2; 6). Ruth was a Moabitess who was also one of the great-grandmothers of Jesus, but having come from Moab, she was considered an outsider and unclean (Ruth). Finally, Bathsheba was the one with whom King David committed adultery, and whose husband, Uriah, King David murdered (2 Samuel 11).

St. Matthew therefore unites Jesus—in His very family line—with women associated with prostitution, ethnic impurity, and adultery. God wants people to know that His Son was sent to save sinners *through* sinners; and Jesus is not ashamed to be close to them. In fact, Jesus desired them to be His family. Is the Gospel inclusive? Yes, because Jesus Himself wanted the world to know He willed to have the lineage He had. This in itself says that Jesus is for all.

In St. Matthew 9, the apostle recorded his own call into the ministry. He did not conceal his former way of life. He was a tax collector. This might seem an innocuous detail, but nothing could be further from the truth. In that culture and at that time, tax collectors were considered among the most notorious of criminals. They were empowered by the local governments to collect taxes, but nothing stopped them from abusing their power. They would overcharge and keep the profits for themselves. They were despised and considered as low as prostitutes on the social scale. As Jesus was eating with tax collectors and other sinners, "The Pharisees [religious elites at the time who guarded God's Law] saw this, [and] they said to His disciples, 'Why does your teacher eat with tax collectors and sinners?'" (Matthew 9:10–11). In response to this critical question, Jesus said, "Those who are well have no need of a physician, but those who are sick. . . . I came not to call the righteous, but sinners" (vv. 12–13).

Once again, Jesus showed that He came to associate with and to serve people who might think they are outside the love of God. Jesus would have nothing to do with the limitation of God's love. If anyone said, "This one does not deserve God's love!" then the Christian faith may legitimately answer, "What does 'deserve' have to do with it?" Instead, the love that Jesus Christ extended was and is boundless.

The pattern in Scripture is unmistakable: Jesus serves a Roman centurion's servant (Luke 7). The centurion, as a Roman officer, was associated with Roman religious pluralism and idolatry. It didn't matter; Jesus included him and healed his servant. In this same chapter, Jesus permits a woman publicly known as a sinner to wash and anoint His feet in front of religious leaders. Jesus didn't care about their judgment; He cared only to show how serious He was to be inclusive about His saving ministry. One of the early followers the Lord Jesus had included was a woman called Mary Magdalene. She had been healed of seven demons. Jesus embraced her disciple-ship and later gave her the honor of being the first to witness His resurrection (Luke 8; John 20).

Luke 15, however, might be the most splendid of God's universal messages about His inclusive love and mercy. The story of the prodigal son came from the lips of Jesus Himself as He sought to communicate the enormity of God's love toward humanity. The prodigal son showed his excessive careless-ness by dishonoring his father in so many ways. He intimated through the demand for his inheritance that he wished his father would hurry up and die; and then he took that inheritance and, wasting it through reckless living, he entered a life of im-purity and disgrace. What would the father do, and who could have blamed him if he decided to disown his injurious son? Yet, when his son returned to beg for mercy, the father, who demonstrates the grace of God, went running to his sinful son, embraced him, and kissed him. For a noble man in that culture, the very action of running in his fine robes would have been taboo, and yet he didn't care. If others judged his tremendous forgiving love, casting aside his son's great shame, he ob-viously couldn't have cared less. All the father cared about was the full restoration of his beloved son. This is how God in Christ loves all people.

In John 4, we have the incredible record of Jesus speak-ing to the Samaritan woman at the well. Again, the cultural context reveals what would otherwise be considered a scan-dalous situation. First of all, good Jews were not supposed to associate with Samaritans, who were viewed by Jews as having compromised their national and religious purity. In the case of Jesus speaking to this woman, this was only the be-ginning of the scandal. Jesus was a rabbi (a teacher), and for a rabbi to be alone with a woman like this was considered inappropriate. Furthermore, this particular woman would have been looked down upon by most everyone in the community. She had been married five times and the man she was with at the time was not her husband. In spite of all these things, Jesus was speaking to her in the middle of the day and out in the open, unafraid of who might see them. The truth could not be hidden: He really did come for all people. Nobody's sin or guilt or shame could keep them from the grace of God through Jesus Christ. Jesus permits no exceptions.

This is the love and unqualified inclusion Christians must bring to the people in front of them. At the same time, Christians must conduct themselves with the further clarity that they dare not compromise the exclusivity of Christ alone for salvation. With this clarity, Christians should never be less than confident about this "both-and" lens of faith. It is not only intelligent and logical, but more important, it is what the Word of God clearly reveals. This truth, therefore, is something to celebrate and not hide. It enables Christians to love all people and, at the same time, offer Jesus Christ alone as the answer to what all need, be they those who confess Jesus Christ and therefore bear the name of Christ, or those who do not. However, this first movement of love—this first lens—is absolutely essential: to love all people so that none are excluded, and to love God so that the Gospel resting on Christ alone is never compromised.

THE NEXT LENS: THOSE WHO FEEL THEIR NEED AND HELPLESSNESS, AND THOSE WHO DO NOT

With this groundwork in place, what is the difference—if any—in applying God's love to those who feel their need and helplessness, and to those who do not? This is a critical question, and we have to carefully answer it, as it touches on the second lens of faith shared in this chapter, about the Gospel's application. As a heads-up, we will look at the message spoken even more carefully in chapter 11, but for now, we need to consider more precisely to whom we are speaking.

We had mentioned above that this next step and next set of lenses—feeling the need for the Gospel and knowing true helplessness or not—is not a matter of labeling people. As a matter of fact, we become aware of where a person is here, not by what we cast or foist on them in terms of labeling them, but rather through what they share about themselves: whether they reveal brokenness or not. That is, this next lens is not a label but a self-disclosure. It is something told by the other, not something stamped on the other.

Why not, however, just stick to what many Christians prefer to talk about at this juncture: *Christians* or *non-Christians*? Aren't we just saying the same thing here? No, not really (and this is not to contradict the true meaning of *Christian* from chapter 3). While it is indeed virtuous to put the best construction on things, this does not mean that we can take at face value what individuals mean when they refer to themselves as "Christian." The term—indeed the label—has taken on a host of meanings. To some it is simply analogous to a general belief in God, so that *Christian* becomes synonymous with *theist*, one who believes in the existence of a personal God. What others mean by the label, however, is closer to *moralist*, one who believes in good over bad behavior. Another might use the term to refer to popular or national religion. In this case, a "Christian" might be someone with a conservative political position who takes pride in referring to the United States as a "Christian nation." Still others might call themselves "Christian" because they believe that Jesus Christ came into the world to show us the way to God by keeping His ethical teachings (even while denying His miracles and saving ministry).

An actual Christian, however, is the one we described

in chapter 3. This is the one who is *in Christ* and belongs to Christ—indeed, is *Christ's*. In particular, the true Christian holds to both who Jesus truly is—true God and true man, God incarnate and God who took on human flesh—and what Jesus truly did to save us from the world, the devil, and our sin: namely, win for us the forgiveness of sins, life, and salvation (recall the specifics in chapter 3). Real Christians cling to the new life that Jesus Christ has given them and lives in and through them.

The accurate description of *Christian* can only really be known in the heart and by God. If we are speaking to others, though, we cannot look into their heart, nor can we—fortunately—read their mind. What is left are the things that can be seen and heard. Even more basic for communicating where people are at, however, is what they disclose about what is in their heart and mind. That is, what do they say of their need for God? What do they say about their security and self-sufficiency? This second lens of faith informs us about how to apply God's love in accord with where people are in their lives, regardless of what they call themselves, and regardless of their outward associations.

In other words, for this second lens of faith, we are seeking to know whether people are concerned about their life, and if they are, then whether they consider the solution to be within their ability. Along the way, we do not make assumptions about people's spiritual status based on whether they attend public worship services, live an upright life, or exhibit any other external sign. These assumptions are cast aside. Instead, we want to know if people feel a personal need for God's help, knowing that they cannot save themselves.

Having said this, we can now take the next step and say that it is impossible for people to feel that they have a need for the Gospel of Jesus Christ if they do not also feel their sin. The Gospel is often compared to a medicine, but why take medicine if they believe they are perfectly healthy? It is only when someone believes that they are sick that they then feel the need for medicine. Those who do not feel the burden of their personal sin will not feel that they need the Savior, Jesus, who came to forgive sinners their sin.

This is another way of saying that true Christians—those who feel their need for the Gospel—also feel very strongly about their sin. They have a clear understanding that they have fallen short of God's standard, which is His good and Holy Law. They feel convicted of their sin, they feel sorrow or contrition over their sins, and they desire to confess their sins to God so that they would know God's consolation through the forgiveness of sins. Then, having been forgiven their sins, they desire to live in consecration to God, living for Him with new joy and commitment to the life of Christ. Then, the next day, this order starts all over again:

1. Conviction

2. Contrition

3. Confession

4. Consolation

5. Consecration

Note, however, where this order *begins*: it begins with knowing that there is a need for the Gospel precisely because they are convicted regarding their sin. On account of feeling their sin, they may then get to the point of feeling their need for the Gospel. We must be careful, however, to understand that the Holy Spirit needs to conduct the transition from conviction and contrition to confession and consolation leading to con-secration. Recall that some can wallow in their sinful struggle; some can become so focused on their sin that they begin to treat it as an idol as they try to convince themselves that their sin is stronger than God's grace. If this happens, misery takes over. This is when the enemy (the devil) convinces people that they are too far gone for the Gospel; but we must remember that the devil is a liar and that instead, the Gospel is always for those who feel the great burden of their sin.

This means, therefore, that those who do not feel the need for the Gospel do not really feel their sin. They might intellectually acknowledge that they sin and may even call themselves "sinner," but this mental acknowledgment is not the same as *feeling* their sin. To feel sin is to know it as a burden. It causes sorrow, it afflicts the conscience, and it leads them to wish they could be rid of it. The soul hates sin and wishes that its condition could be something other than what it is. God's goal, then, is that these same people would despair of their own ability, and desire help for their sin. It is a good thing when this happens; then they want to be healed even while knowing that they can't heal themselves.

However, how do people come to this conviction about sin? There is only one way: through the Law of God. Introducing God's Law to those who do not yet feel their need for the Gospel is not unloving; it is the only way to properly love these people at this juncture. Consider again the analogy of being sick: how good and faithful would a doctor be if he or she diagnosed a life-threatening disease but decided not to inform the patient, even when there was a way of treating the disease and saving the patient's life? A doctor who withheld such information, as hard as it would be for the patient to hear, would be considered an evil doctor indeed.

When someone shares that they feel no need for God's help, then they need one loving service: they need someone to share God's Law with them, because the Law of God is that which reveals sin. This is a major revelation to some on account of the extremely popular notion that God's Law was not given to show sin but to show how we might save ourselves by keeping the Law. That is, the purpose of God's Law is often missed. However, God Himself says, "Through the law comes knowledge of sin" (Romans 3:20). The split second it is known that a person does not feel that he or she needs the Gospel—whether that person is the president of a Christian congregation, a pastor, a criminal, or a person who has never set foot in a church—then that person needs to hear God's Law. Much more will be said about this in chapter 11.

For now, however, we simply need to know this: those who feel their need for God's intervention and have forsaken their own solutions apart from God should immediately hear the Gospel; but if they do not feel their need for the Gospel, then they need to hear the Law of God first. Until they feel the great burden of their sin and their helplessness to save themselves, they will feel no need for the Gospel, which at this point will seem empty and irrelevant.

I was always close my father, who was about forty years my senior. My love for him ran deep; I looked up to him, and I was proud to be his son. Nevertheless, I lived my life for many years knowing that my dad seemed unclear about the Gospel and, for the most part, did not appear to be urgent about it. For the longest time, I wasn't sure if he believed he really needed it. We had many conversations about the Gospel, and for that matter, I wrote him several letters over the years, but I remained uncertain about his position. All of that changed in a moment of time.

My dad and other family members came out to surprise me for my fortieth birthday. It was indeed a great surprise since at the time, I was living far away from my folks. I was ecstatic to see them and we quickly made plans about how to spend our time together. We decided, among other things, to venture to a downtown museum where an exciting tour of the Vatican was on display. We were all looking forward to this family outing, and we agreed that it would be interesting. I had no idea what was about to happen, and it turned out to be nothing short of an answered prayer.

While several members of the family attended the outing, for whatever reason, I got paired up with my dad. He couldn't walk very fast, so I held back to stay with him and to soak in our time together. It was thoroughly enjoyable, and I was also having fun using my theological training to shed some light here and there about the religious symbolism that marked our paths. I would have never predicted what was about to happen next. My dad and I came across a scaled-down reproduction of Michelangelo's *The Last Judgment*. We were fascinated by being so close to the spectacular fresco, and it wasn't long before I realized that my dad was completely mesmerized by it. I had never before seen him demonstrate such a visceral reaction to any art, but on this day, he was glued to the symbol of the Last Judgment.

After standing there for some time, the pace of our tour now having been thoroughly interrupted, I started to look back and forth between my dad's face and the painting. I was trying to read him, and he appeared to have a look of perplexity, perhaps even of concern. I decided to jump in.

> "So, Dad, this is a visual representation of what is taught in the Word of God at St. Matthew, chapter 25. The Word of God says that the Lord—who is pictured here at center in glory—will come again with His angels and He will separate the people one from another as a shepherd separates the sheep from the goats. He will put the sheep on His right hand and the goats on His left. Notice the expression of those on His right. They have the look of relief and joy—they are the ones who are secure at His right side—and they are called 'sheep' because they

listened to the Lord's voice while they lived on earth and followed Him. Now look at the ones on His left. Their expressions are completely different. Note the expressions of fear and dread. See how on the one side, they are being raised up, and on the other, they are being pulled down. It is an amazing depiction of God's Word concerning the Last Judgment that occurs, of course, on the Last Day."

I finished my cursory summary and continued to notice that my dad hadn't really changed his expression. Then he finally spoke. His words slowly dragged out of his mouth, and I had never heard him so concerned about things pertaining to the Christian faith. He said—slowly and deliberately, with much feeling and alarm—"But I thought that all people were going to heaven." In a flash, I realized that I had just heard what had been a blockade to all my previous efforts to talk to him about the Gospel. For all these years, my father had assumed and believed in a form of universalism, which, by definition, does not worry about the problem of sin in relation to salvation. He had believed that regardless of what people believed in or how people lived, they would end up in heaven. Now, while standing in front of this fresco with a short talk on Matthew 25, all that changed. My dad was now very interested in his standing before God.

It was the Lord who had opened a door that evidently had never been opened, and I was able to walk through it by sharing the Gospel with my dad on the spot. I followed up in response to his expressed need for help and his expressed anxiety about his sin and whether his sin might put him among those on the left of Christ in the painting. I proceeded to share with him about what Jesus had done for the sins of the world and what those on Jesus' right in the fresco knew. I explained why they looked upon Him with confidence and familiar expectation. I explained to my dad why they were on Jesus' right side, all because of what Jesus had done for them through His life, death, and resurrection. My father had never been so attentive in a conversation about faith, ever. I was beside myself about what had just happened.

Needless to say, I was very interested in what would happen next. My dad was quiet on the ride back to my place. It took about an hour to get home. When we arrived, my dad made a beeline to the master bedroom, where he and my mom were staying. He evidently wanted to be alone. Everyone respected his wishes. I'm not sure how much time went by before he came out of the room, but when he did, I saw something in my dad I had simply never witnessed. He came out, evidently having read a gospel magazine in my bedroom, and his face was shining.

Then, something amazing happened. For the first time in my life—and keep in mind that I was forty and my dad was eighty—I heard my father quote Holy Scripture. He walked out into the living room and announced exuberantly, "Did you know that the Good Book says, 'Greater love has no one than this, that someone lay down his life for his friends'?" (John 15:13). I knew after our earlier conversation around the fresco that my dad knew who had laid down His life for him and for everyone else. The Holy Spirit had shown my dad his great need, and he had come to believe what God in Christ had done about it. The Gospel was inclusive—it included *him*—and it was exclusive, pointing him to Jesus. Now, he could not hold back his great relief. Six years later, when my dad was preparing to enter into glory, he held to Christ and knew his sins had been forgiven. My dad had come to feel his need for the Gospel, and the Good News came into his possession.

DISCUSSION GUIDE:

THE LUTHERAN LENS—TO WHOM AM I SPEAKING?

Uncover Information

1. What do we mean by saying that the Gospel is both *inclusive* and *exclusive*?

2. According to 1 John 4:8 and 16, *what* is God?

3. Which one is true? "Faith makes the Gospel effective"; or, "The Gospel makes faith effective."

4. How does John 14:6 support the exclusivity of the Gospel?

5. When is a person ready to hear the Gospel?

Discover Meaning

1. What kind or type of love is expressed in John 3:16?

2. Refer to Romans 5:6, 8, 10 to discuss how 1 John 4:8, 16 is not an abstraction but something that we can begin to understand. Describe this love in view of Romans 5.

3. Test yourself: if the Gospel is universal, then God loves the hardened criminal as much as He loves you. Do you believe it? Why or why not?

4. Why is exclusivity necessary for inclusivity?

5. Why does readiness for hearing the Gospel include both acknowledging need *and* helplessness? We are saying that people need to admit that not only are they sinners, but also that they can do nothing to save themselves. Why are both important?

EXPLORE IMPLICATIONS

1. If God has loved us this way, how should the Christian respond? Please elaborate, because this is much easier said than done. How can this happen?

2. This love of God makes His *grace* (His love and mercy that saves) *universal*. Discuss implications of this: you can walk up to *anyone* (regardless of status, lifestyle, or your natural affection or lack thereof for that person), and God loves them, period!

3. Review the list of Scriptures on universal grace in this chapter as quoted from the Lutheran Confessions. How should this impact the way we live?

4. Review the basic arguments for why exclusivity and inclusivity are not contradictory. How can understanding this produce confidence for sharing the Gospel with others?

5. Discuss the "Five Cs" in this chapter. Why should these be a daily thing in the life of the Christian?

CHAPTER 9

THE LUTHERAN LENS—
WHERE ARE WE?

Christians are citizens of and constantly live in two realms or kingdoms: the earthly society under government (the so-called *kingdom of the left* or *kingdom of power*) and life in the Church (the so-called *kingdom of the right* or *kingdom of grace*). That is, every Christian holds dual citizenship: they are citizens of their earthly country, and citizens of a grace kingdom that will find fulfillment in a "better country" (Hebrews 11:16), a heavenly one. Christians live their lives in these two realms and are always present in them. Both kingdoms are going on at the same time, and the Christian is active in both at the same time. This is the essential lens of faith we must be aware of regarding where the Christian is, or rather where the Christian lives. The Lutheran Confessions teach on these two kingdoms:

> Therefore, our teachers, in order to comfort people's consciences, were constrained to show the difference between the authority of the Church and the authority of the State. They taught that both of them are to be held in reverence and honor, as God's chief blessings on earth, because they have God's command.[34]

---

34   AC XXVIII 4.

CHURCH AND STATE

We must carefully consider the terminology, because in the popular way of speaking in the culture and politics, people speak of "church and state." The two frames of reference— kingdom of power and kingdom of grace on the one hand, and church and state on the other—while similar, are not the same thing. It is important, however, to keep both sets of dualities in front of us, because while the two "kingdoms" provide deeper biblical understanding about where we live, "church and state" helps us to keep up with the popular discussion.

Before jumping into more important details, let's compare and coordinate the two sets of dualities. "Kingdom of power" and "government and state" are indeed similar. What is often missing in the "state" concept that the theological kingdom includes, however, is that "government" is not merely formal government (e.g., the executive, legislative, and judicial branches of government in the United States); but the theological kingdom of power includes all the various hierarchies in the culture (apart from the Church), including the vital one of family. Fathers and mothers, for example, are crucial examples of the kingdom of power. Thus, when the culture talks about the "state," its definition is limited.

Similarly, the "kingdom of grace"—or the kingdom of the Church—is not in exact alignment with what the culture means by "church." The theological kingdom of the Church is invisible and is not strapped down to a visible institution. Luther, in his famous *The Bondage of the Will*, wrote, "The Church is hidden, the saints are unknown."[35] Elsewhere, Luther said that even the Christian is hidden from himself.[36] The Church is always where King Jesus exerts His power to save from the world, the devil, and our sin through His Word and Sacraments. Jesus

---

35   AE 33:89.
36   AE 35:411.

therefore said this about His kingdom to His disciples: "The kingdom of God is in the midst of you" (Luke 17:21). That is, the Lord's kingdom cannot be walled in and reduced to an earthly institution. The Church cannot be limited this way.

The discussion about "church" in the cultural dialogue, however, very much treats "church" as an institution. This is understandable. After all, from the standpoint of human observation, people see human organizations represented in the myriad of denominations and so forth. Most concretely, people physically gather in local congregations. When the culture, therefore, tries to limit the voice of the "church" in the public square, it might seem like a reasonable argument, but the problem is that the concept of church is significantly reduced. Christians as members of the Church, however, are always *in Christ* and carry the Word of Christ with them wherever they go. Christians never cease to operate apart from their faith, even in the so-called "public square," which many want to limit to state matters only. It is always important for the Christian to know when the public square discussion spills over into matters of faith, and if it does, how to respond to it.

CHRISTIANS IN THE PUBLIC SQUARE

For example, defending religious liberty is a crucial task for Christians today that must be addressed in the public square. The great irony of those trying to limit the Christian voice in the public square is that they, too, have a religious worldview when "religion" includes any position about God. When Christians debate atheists about these matters, it is not that one side is religious and the other is not. Rather, both parties hold theological viewpoints. One says that God exists, and the other says God does not exist. Both belief systems about God easily influence what follows in their respective ethics and morality. These, in turn, further impact the culture for all people.

On account of these things, the Christian should never step away from the public square. If they do, they permit others to set the cultural agenda for the place in which they live. Anyone trying to influence the culture while maintaining that they do so in religious neutrality is either being deceptive or just doesn't know any better. Such activism never takes place in a theological vacuum. Everyone believes in something, even if they say they believe in nothing. Faith convictions and their expressions abound. It takes faith to believe in nothing and in the many other objects of faith that are too many to list.

Responding to the culture in the public square is the challenging part, and it can come in different forms. First of all, it is entirely possible to effectively respond by emulating the example of St. Paul. Paul ventured to Athens and found himself at the Areopagus, where legal cases were argued. This was an environment of the state, not the church. What St. Paul did, however, was ingenious (and certainly inspired by the Holy Spirit). He found a way to connect to the elite crowd by bridging the biblical teaching on creation to the altar dedicated to "the unknown god" (Acts 17:23). From this launching point, St. Paul went on to proclaim Christ as the risen one. Even in this state setting—in this public square—St. Paul found a way to connect the Gospel to his audience. The Lord still opens doors for this to happen if His Christians are only willing to speak.

Second, sometimes the Christian is provided golden opportunities to give answer to assaults against marriage, life, and family through the resource of natural law. This is also from God and is something that any human being should be able to relate to regardless of religion, worldview, or ideology. As Christians continue to consult the breadth of God's revelation, part of that revelation includes what God has given to all people in accord with what is known intuitively by conscience or through observation of creation. This is what we mean by *natural law*. This knowledge is built into the experience of being a human being on planet earth. Such knowledge also comes from God, though many try to deny it. The Word of God teaches:

> For when Gentiles, who do not have the law, by nature do what the law requires, they are a law to themselves, even though they do not have the law. They show that the work of the law is written on their hearts, while their conscience also bears witness, and their conflicting thoughts accuse or even excuse them. (Romans 2:14–15)

While the Christian might use special revelation in the public square (similar to what St. Paul did at Athens, speaking about the creation and resurrection of Christ), he or she can also use natural revelation or law. Christians just need to know how to use it. For example, many non-Christians assert that babies should be aborted. There is a natural-law response that focuses on the personhood or the humanity of the unborn baby. If murdering a person is wrong, and if a baby is a person, then murdering a baby is wrong. It is the task of natural law to demonstrate that unborn babies are in fact human. Along the way, a natural-law argument does not need special revelation, nor does it need to quote chapter and verse in the Bible. If a non-Christian argues that same-sex unions should be permitted marriage, here, again, the Christian can respond with natural law. Marriage naturally includes male and female, and these are in fact legitimate categories—beyond religion and tradition—within the species. That is, genders are not sociological constructs, but rather are indicative of what human beings are by nature.

In summary, as we describe the Christian in the public square, we see that a Christian might speak up according to special revelation or natural law. Both should be considered legitimate options that counter extreme ideas of the separation of church and state. Christians are citizens in this culture, and they have a right to speak—and they should.

Are we saying, however, that public speaking and debate is the only way that Christians engage the culture? Is the key to our living in the world having ready philosophical arguments or theological oratories? Should we start to enroll in college courses on the philosophy of religion and natural law? We could, and that would be great, but there is much more the Christian needs to be aware of. Even as Christians should always be ready to give an answer for their faith (1 Peter 3:15), God has arranged for a living testimony of faith that comes through the way His Christians live.

AS BAD AS THE STATE REALM
MIGHT BE, IT IS STILL GOOD

How, then, should Christians live? The position that Christians become isolationists will not do. We cannot leave the world. We cannot pretend that the culture we live in doesn't exist. It is too important to God and it should be important to the Christian as well. The people for whom Jesus lived, died, and rose make up the culture. God wants Christians in the culture. Jesus said that Christians are salt and light in the world (Matthew 5:13–14). The question, therefore, is exactly how do Christians relate to the culture in which they live? Once again, we need the lens of faith to help. It comes through a proper understanding of "church and state" as it is tempered and qualified by the biblical and confessional teaching about the kingdom of power and the kingdom of grace.

Because the terminology of "church and state" intersects (to a degree) with the two biblical kingdoms, we must maintain the legitimate differences. Jesus taught, "My kingdom is not of this world" (John 18:36), while refusing to merge God's kingdom for salvation with the government. In another instance when His enemies were trying to trap Him, He said, "Render to Caesar the things that are Caesar's, and to God the things that are God's" (Matthew 22:21). By saying this, Jesus was not implying that the things belonging to Caesar exist apart from God. Still, the two realms are not to be confused. They remain distinct and separate.

God is, however, still in control of the state realm. When Jesus was being interrogated by Pilate before being sentenced to crucifixion, Pilate spoke down to Jesus and said, "You will not speak to me? Do You not know that I have authority to release You and authority to crucify You?" (John 19:10). Pilate, however, had gone too far in saying this. Recall, there are things unseen. Jesus replied, "You would have no authority over Me at all unless it had been given you from above" (v. 11). Apart from Christ, Pilate had no power.

Both kingdoms—the kingdom of God's grace known in the Church and the kingdom of God's power known in political government—belong to God, are of God, and accomplish good. God works through both. It is just that they serve different purposes through different means. St. Paul provided important insight about the political realm that we typically refer to as "the state":

> Let every person be subject to the governing authorities. For there is no authority except from God, and those that exist have been instituted by God. Therefore whoever resists the authorities resists what God has appointed, and those who resist will incur judgment. For rulers are not a terror to good conduct, but to bad. Would you have no fear of the one who is in authority? Then do what is good, and you will receive his approval, for he is God's servant for your good. But if you do wrong, be afraid, for he does not bear the sword in vain. For he is the servant of God, an avenger who carries out God's wrath on the wrongdoer. Therefore one

must be in subjection, not only to avoid God's wrath but also for the sake of conscience. For because of this you also pay taxes, for the authorities are ministers of God, attending to this very thing. (Romans 13:1–6)

The political realm therefore is an immensely good thing. It is, in spite of all its problems, of God and therefore holy. As the Word of God says, the political authorities are "ministers of God," that is, they are servants of God whether they know it or not. Having been instituted by God, these are, again, holy. With all the corruption that exists in the realm of politics, this seems outlandish, and yet it is still true. Anything that is holy is set apart by God. God appoints holy things and God works through holy things for His purposes and in His time. The state is also God's.

One of the most powerful examples of this truth pertains to the history of the people of Israel. They had lost everything when they were deported to Babylon and were subjugated to the Babylonian power. How could they in a million years ever be able to return to the Promised Land? Being among the people of God during this time must have been extraordinarily disheartening. The people of Israel were once the zenith of civilization, especially under David and Solomon, and slavery in Egypt was ancient history, but they found themselves in exile again. Being so far away from home and so helpless to do anything about it, what could possibly offer them hope? Answer: the state.

The Babylonians were taken over by the Persians, and King Cyrus was the man in charge. This powerful king did not know the Lord. This, however, did not stop the Lord from acting through him. The Scriptures say, "The LORD stirred up the spirit of Cyrus king of Persia," and the rest is history (Ezra 1:1). Cyrus decided that it was best to permit the Israelites to return to their land and so they did. God had decided to work through Cyrus, and Cyrus became God's chosen instrument through his position as a political king.

> [God said] of Cyrus, "He is My shepherd, and he shall fulfill all My purpose"; saying of Jerusalem, "She shall be built," and of the temple, "Your foundation shall be laid." (Isaiah 44:28)

What Nebuchadnezzar, king of Babylon, destroyed, Cyrus, king of Persia, would (indirectly) rebuild. Working through him, though, was God. Remember what Jesus had said to Pilate? The same was true in the Old Testament and the same is true today: the state would have no power unless given it from above. Why does God give power to the state? For His will to be done and for good to be had. Again, we are tempted to shake our heads and exclaim, "How can this be? Don't you see the terrible things going on in the world today?" This is where we return to the theology of the cross. God is still working even when it appears He is nowhere to be seen, and He will continue to work good for His people. We may not be able to see this with our physical eyes, but we can see this with the eyes of faith.

Still, Persia did not become Israel, and Israel did not become Persia. The account of King Cyrus does not imply that the president of the United States should be a Christian nor that culture in the United States should be transformed into a so-called "Christian culture." This calls for a balanced view and the reminder that the Lord said (in fact, in this verse He said it twice), "My kingdom is not of this world" (John 18:36). Jesus calls His people—His Christians—to be salt and light, but He never said that the culture itself should be the Church, nor that the Church should become the culture. That there is a distinction between church and state is not just something political scientists maintain; more importantly, God does. This insight can be incredibly liberating for the Christian.

MERGING CHURCH AND STATE
—SOMETHING TO AVOID

Liberation comes when Christians no longer confuse church and state by assuming that God has called them to transform the culture. When Christians insist on cultural transformation, unsavory and complex projects ensue: either Christians try to find ways to turn secular institutions into Christian ones, or for every secular institution, a parallel Christian institution is built. Not only are fantastic amounts of resources required for such projects, but considerable resources are lost toward serving the culture in the proper way. When the wrong projects are abandoned, then Christians have freedom to live in simpler and more effective ways. God's way still says, "My kingdom is not of this world" (John 18:36).

Too many Christians and certain Christian traditions, however, instead of embracing the freedom that comes with this proper distinction, have preferred to bind themselves to the view that church and state should merge. Too many Christians have presumed that their role is to convert the culture. Such an agenda, however, comes with many problems. One of them is that while the Word of the Lord never changes, the culture is always changing. Trying to combine these is like mixing oil and water. It doesn't work. Unfortunately, what ends up happening too often is that the convictions of the faith become watered down. The pull of power in politics will often lead to theological and ethical compromise. There are reasons for maintaining the distinction, and one of the most important ones is that the Church serves the state as a salve and conscience. Once the Church tries to marry the state, however, the Church will begin to lose her identity and in time will become a subcategory of the state.

At this juncture, two messages come forth. One message is that the Christian should be active in the culture, be salt and light, and be used by God to positively affect the culture. The other message is that the Christian mustn't confuse the Church with the state, maintaining a clear distinction. This balance is the first step in living with this church-and-state lens of faith.

The question now becomes, what do we mean by a Christian living actively in the culture as salt and light without confusing the Church with the culture? As a first step toward answering this question, recall that the state and the culture it oversees should be viewed as being holy. This view should be maintained since these are established by God. God works through the state and the culture it serves in spite of any crass inconsistencies with His Holy Word. These are still to be viewed as holy, set apart for the purposes of God, and more than worthy of the Christian's full participation and interaction. God would not have it any other way.

THE CHRISTIAN IN HOLY VOCATION

With this holiness of the culture in place—in spite of its terrible inconsistencies—we may take the next step and understand that the *vocations*, or callings, within the culture are also holy. Such a view changes everything. Luther said, "Every occupation has its own honor before God, as well as its own requirements and duties."[37] Too often people do not see this. Once again, we are taken back to the things seen and unseen. People don't get God's way. God views all vocations as holy, because they come from Him. Luther again: "All the estates and works of God are to be praised as highly as they can be, and none despised in favor of another."[38]

This is not just a theological factoid. If this truth of God is believed, then everything in our attitude about vocation

---

37   AE 46:246.
38   AE 46:246.

should change. These are not just jobs or roles, but they are callings from God, holy things, and ways to serve God and neighbor. As God worked through Cyrus to help Israel, God works through people in holy vocation so that others may benefit and be served. God is the one working through holy vocation, so every vocation becomes extraordinarily important.

Many Christians are influenced by a false spirituality that they must somehow be "more Christian" in their vocation by maintaining a higher standard of the law, by using Christian phrases, or by being more overt in appearing religious or spiritual. Certainly, we can never pray too much, nor should we forget to look for chances to witness more openly when the opportunity presents itself. Along the way, however, it is easy to forget what God has already done to help us live in our faith in a way that does not call for extraordinary feats, but rather through the simple lens that sees vocations as holy.

Since God has made being an administrative assistant holy, then one should aspire to be the best admin he or she can be. As God has made being a security guard holy, then being faithful as a security guard gives glory to God. Christian attorneys ought to be invigorated to know that God works through them to help others. Christian doctors may rejoice that they're extensions of the healing hands of God. Christian teachers faithful to their calling impart knowledge to equip people, helping lives. This is God's work. Christian artists should desire to glorify the Maker of all things, even as their work may testify to the Creator Himself. Knowing that being a mother or father is holy, then we should be confident that God is with us to glorify Him as we strive to be the best parent possible. Christian grandparents should resolve to be a blessing for their grandchildren, knowing fully that God works through them in a vocation that is completely unique. When Christians make it their goal to be the best students, athletes, workers, or citizens they can be—whatever they are—then they will live with eyes of faith on God: "And whatever you do, in word or deed, do everything in the name of the Lord Jesus, giving thanks to God the Father through Him" (Colossians 3:17).

Having said all of this on vocation, it should be made clear that there is no inference here that excellence in vocation means an excuse to live in silence about the Word of God. In other words, this is not an "either-or," but true to our lens treatment, a "both-and." Faithfulness in vocation makes it easier to be in the position to share the Gospel. The Christian should take full advantage of this situation. The Christian seeks to live and speak the Gospel. Both are needed and very much complementary. If someone observes a Christian truly devoted to service, then anything that Christian says will hold more weight with the listener.

If we indeed achieve a standard of excellence in what we are called to do, then we earn the respect of those around us. Excellence in vocation gives a person a voice. Here, we become cognizant of another duality important to remember: while our relationship with God does not depend on what we do but rather depends on faith, our relationship with people very much depends on what we do. Through faith, we are justified by God. Through works, we are justified by people. God looks at the heart; people look at our works. If our conduct and work are outstanding, we are often granted a platform, we earn respect, we gain an audience; people are more apt to want to know us, and they will be more apt to care about what we say. People who have good reputations are permitted a leeway that those without good reputations never know. An outstanding reputation earns an air of authority or at least respectability that can open doors. If this is what we achieve through faithfulness and hard work in vocation, then it will be ten times easier to be a witness for Jesus Christ.

My friend Doug is the president and CEO of the company he has worked extraordinarily hard to build. He started out with his first restaurant in the 1980s, and it has blossomed into a very recognizable brand in Southern California. He has by the grace of God built an outstanding reputation in the industry, and he has done it while seeking God. Doug is an example of being the best he can be to the glory of God. His entrepreneurship has included leveraging his success in business to be a blessing to the Church and her mission. There are too many examples of his dedication for spreading the Gospel than can be cited, but there is one in particular that makes me smile every time I think about it. He called and asked if we could get together for breakfast. What did he want to talk about? I'm always intrigued when it comes to my brother in Christ Doug.

Like clockwork, we talk about faith and family, and this morning was no different. We both love holy vocation and so we share our time in giving updates about being husbands and fathers, sons and brothers. Of course, we also get to what we do professionally, and he has been there to encourage me over the years, but it is also common for me to serve him pastorally and provide spiritual counsel. This time, his request was especially fun and exciting. "Pastor, I'm thinking about putting Scripture verses on the inside of the bottom rims of my restaurant cups. I need some recommendations." Most of our time that morning was used for brainstorming Bible passages, but behind the conversation was how we might introduce the Word of God to people in a way that would draw them to the Word. Who knows? The simple encounter with a Scripture on a cup might be the first step toward someone getting to know Jesus. He jotted down my several recommendations and ended up choosing some of them for his cups.

The Lord put Doug in this position, and Doug has run with

it. He has not tried to be hyperspiritual. He has not tried too hard to be something he isn't, but he has embraced what God has made him to be. He has relished living in holy vocation and has used his vocations to give glory to God and to testify to His Word. Having been faithful in vocation, he has been permitted by God to do more with His gifts to give witness to faith. This is exactly the pattern every Christian should try to emulate: just be faithful in what God has made you to be, and doors for witnessing will open; faith will be permitted to shine naturally.

All Christians have this call from God. This is what *vocation* means, and it is from the Latin *vocare*. It means "to call." God calls us to be a blessing to others. When by the grace of God we are faithful in holy vocation, what *we* do as God works through us is more impactful than we realize. Faithfulness in vocation, for example, can also be yet another testimony to *natural law*. We started this chapter talking about the need to defend religious liberty, but the way in which we may impact the culture surpasses anything that can be accomplished by attending a public rally or march (though these, too, can be very good things). What we can really do is be faithful in holy vocation.

The reason defending religious liberty is so vital is because of what is at stake, namely, marriage, life, and the family. Religious liberty gives us the ability to speak in the public square for these vital rudiments of what it means to live out the Christian faith. We cannot forget, however, that our "speaking" is also (not only) heard in our actions, what we do. In Christians' personal expressions of religious liberty, they can speak up loud and clear to the rest of the culture. What about marriage, which is under terrible assault in the culture? The Christian in the vocation of holy marriage has a chance to preach this sermon: faithfulness, for ten years, for twenty years, or for fifty, if the Lord grants. What does this say to the world? We cannot overestimate the impact of such faithfulness to the world. Such commitment says marriage is real, marriage is good, and it says to the world that it is worth fighting for. The Christian faithful in marriage can preach a better sermon than a dynamic pastor who defends it from the pulpit.

Angela is another faithful Christian I know who is a professional counselor. She is faithful in living out her commitment to the Lord Jesus Christ through maintaining her standards to be an excellent therapist. When she is in the middle of doing her craft, her focus is on what she has been trained to do and what she has experienced over the years while doing her work. Through faith, she is serving God; in love, she is serving her clients. Because she is an excellent therapist, people trust her and open up to her. She earns the right and is granted the ability to help and make a difference. In this process, Angela also looks for ways to help people in their faith. When natural intersections arrive between psychotherapy and faith—and when clients grant permission for information on other resources—Angela will sometimes recommend my services. On one occasion, one of those referrals led to an extraordinary opportunity for the Gospel to serve holy matrimony. It all happened because Angela was committed to holy vocation, and in this case, marriage was defended and preserved.

Lynn was a committed congregant and regularly attended Divine Service, but one never knew exactly who would be sitting next to her in church, because she had a lot of children in her life. She was an extraordinary foster mother at a time when there were about fifty thousand foster kids in Los Angeles County. Her vocation as foster mother was like a bright light in the congregation. I could teach defending life until I turned blue, but I could never match Lynn's real-life testimony. Her faithfulness in holy vocation spoke volumes to everyone in the congregation and had a direct impact on the culture. It said, "Children are a gift from God and they should have the right to live." Because of her, others in the congregation became foster parents.

At another congregation, we had developed an intentional life ministry and started to participate in something called 40 Days for Life. About once per quarter, volunteers from my congregation and I would meet with other Christians to pray for the unborn and their families at various Planned Parenthood locations. Our presence was peaceable, and if given a chance to put some information on alternative services into the hands of those entering Planned Parenthood, we did so. In between, we were literally in the Word of God and prayer. One afternoon while we were singing hymns and praying on the street just off the sidewalk, a woman came up to me and asked if she could join us. I smiled at her and welcomed her. It was great to have someone from the community stand alongside us. I soon found out that there was a little more going on.

Brenda not only wanted to pray with us, she also desired that we pray for her. We started conversing and she was excited to tell me about her son. She loved him and was fantastically proud. He had been a joy to raise, he worked hard in school, and he went on to become an attorney. Brenda beamed about her son, and I soon realized that based on her experience of having raised a child, there was a reason for her coming out to join us: Brenda believed in the sanctity of life; it was worth defending. But Brenda wasn't finished sharing.

Before she had her wonderful son, she had also once had a daughter in her womb, but she chose to have an abortion. The floodgates opened as she shared her broken heart for what she had done. If her son had turned out as he did, what would have happened if she had allowed her daughter to live? She imagined that her daughter would have had a great life just like her son. Brenda was living with an almost unbearable burden full of guilt, regret, and shame. What had she done? It was time for Jesus to speak to her. She felt her need for the Gospel and was fully aware of her sin. For anyone like Brenda, Jesus still speaks through His Word: "Come to Me, all who labor and are heavy laden, and I will give you rest" (Matthew 11:28). I was ready to share the sweet Gospel with my new friend and sister.

Brenda was crying and once again felt the weight of her past coming down on her. Right there on the street in front of Planned Parenthood, she fell to her knees and pleaded for help and grace. I knelt in front of her and shared with her about the gift of Holy Absolution, when the forgiveness of sins is personally extended to the one desiring it. She agreed to receive it. In the name of the Lord Jesus Christ and by His authority, I pronounced His forgiveness upon Brenda in the name of the Father and of the Son and of the Holy Spirit. I proceeded to pray with her, giving thanks and praise to the Father for her total and complete forgiveness, and then I prayed for our help to always commend her unborn daughter to Him, the one who sent His Son, Jesus; Jesus, who took up the little children in His arms and blessed them (Mark 10:16). That was the first and last day I saw Brenda. She has no idea how much she blessed me. She had courage to confess what she needed to confess, and she showed me just how precious the Gospel is to those in need of it. These were relationships in vocation on a day I got to be a friend and pastor, and on a day when a mother spoke lovingly about her children and became my friend and sister in Christ.

Christians, however, are effective in living out their faith in holy vocation precisely because the powerful Word of God has been given to them. The Christian-disciple-priest is always in possession of the Word. Luther taught that for Christians, God's Word "pervades all [their] works and words and thoughts, [their] heart and body and soul."[39] Luther's elaboration reminds us of how much the Word itself sanctifies holy vocation:

> If you are a manual laborer, you find that the Bible has been put into your workshop, into your hand, into your heart. It teaches and preaches how you should treat your neighbor. Just look at your tools—at your needle or thimble, your beer barrel, your goods, your scales or yardstick or measure—and you will read this statement inscribed on them. Everywhere you look, it stares at you. Nothing that you handle every day is so tiny that it does not continually tell you this, if you will only listen. Indeed, there is no shortage of preaching. You have as many preachers as you have transactions, goods, tools, and other equipment in your house and home. All this is continually crying out to you: "Friend, use me in your relations with your neighbor just as you would want your neighbor to use his property in his relations with you."[40]

Luther understood that God has placed all vocations into *orders* or *institutions*. The church realm is especially represented by the office of priest, while the state realm takes form both through the family and government.[41] The first one is what we normally identify as "church." The second one is what we normally refer to as "state" in the fuller sense of the kingdom of power. What are these for? Luther's description emphasizes the life of faith that must be expressed in love:

> Above these three institutions and orders [that compose the two kingdoms] is the common order of Chris-

---

39   AE 21:237.
40   AE 21:237.
41   AE 37:364–65.

tian love, in which one serves not only the three orders, but also serves every needy person in general
with all kinds of benevolent deeds, such as feeding the
hungry, giving drink to the thirsty, forgiving enemies,
praying for all men on earth, suffering all kinds of evil
on earth, etc. Behold, all of these are called good and
holy works.[42]

TWO KINDS OF WORKS

These are the works, of course, that testify to Christ. Here
we should ensure that we have a proper understanding of the
interplay between the two kingdoms when it comes to the life
of the Christian. In the last quote above, Luther was describing
the Christian ("Christian love") in both realms. In other words,
the Christian has both works: works in the state realm and
works in the church realm. What is more, these can happen simultaneously through the same work. It is possible, therefore,
that one work (like feeding the hungry) can be counted by God
as two different kinds of works done at the same time. How
does that work? The two distinct realms help us to understand.

In the state realm, what makes a work good is the fulfilling
of the duties of a vocation. That is, in the state realm, a work is
good as defined by keeping the law. If a mother is supposed
to change her baby's diapers and does so, then that mother,
whether she is a Christian or not, performs a good work. How
is it good? For one, there is an immediate benefit to another
person; but even more, it is a work that God has commanded (parents must care for their children), enabled, and works
through. As a result, the baby benefits from the fresh diaper.
Again, such a work—the good work in the realm of the state—
is good because it does what vocation is supposed to do.
Since the state is holy by being established by God and since

42   AE 37:365. Brackets added.

the vocations are also holy, then the works within these vocations are holy too. So, Luther also said, "The godless may have much about them that is holy without being saved."[43] This is completely true. The good works in the civil realm benefit people, and God is always behind those works.

In the church realm, however, what makes a work good is not the work itself, but faith in Jesus Christ. Faith is the true fount and source of love, so to do a work in faith is to do a work in love. When this happens, the work itself—and whether it keeps the law—is not the focus. Instead, the work is done for the sake of the person who is loved. The preoccupation is on loving the person served; it is not about being driven by duty. It is easy to slide into a discussion about motivation here, but we are trying not to reduce this to a matter of psychology. When love takes over, what fills the heart and mind surpasses psychology. The love produced by the Holy Spirit is so powerful that all the Christian cares about is the person he or she loves. At this point, a Christian loses track of the cost. He or she cares less about the cost. Love takes on a life of its own, and the Christian begins to do what he or she does simply out of love for the one being served.

Because there are two types of works, it is possible for Christians to do a work that fits the qualifications of both realms. Since it is executed and meets the criterion of having fulfilled a duty, the work itself meets the standard of good work in society; but if that same work is driven by faith and love, then that work is also a good work of the Church and Holy Spirit.

Now we can consider the other side of the lens of faith under discussion. There is another place Christians find themselves.

---

43   AE 37:365.

THE CHRISTIAN'S NEED TO BE IN DIVINE SERVICE

For Christians to be enabled to do works of faith and love—or works of the Church—they need the ministry that is conducted by the Church. Why? Because the work of the Church itself is to give Christians the means and nourishment by which their faith is preserved and caused to grow. Without these means and over time, a Christian's faith could die. This leads us to why it is so important for a Christian to be in church. The Christian's time and commitment to Christ are experienced in Christ's Body (1 Corinthians 12), His Church.

While the invisible Church can never be reduced to a human institution, it is nevertheless also found wherever Jesus' Word and Sacraments are faithfully distributed and received. That is, the Christian needs to be fed, and God gives His Church to feed His Christians. This is the other place in the world that Christians can be found. The writer to the Hebrews is bold in his admonition that Christians should "not [be] neglecting to meet together, as is the habit of some, but encouraging one another, and all the more as you see the Day drawing near" (Hebrews 10:25).

Unfortunately, too many go to church for the wrong reasons. One bad reason is for the sake of information transfer. In this case, the church is viewed pragmatically. The church in this scenario simply safeguards the teaching of Christ, but once a Christian achieves a certain level of proficiency in doctrine, then there is less urgency to be in church. In this case, the church is treated as a learning center. This view is sadly misinformed. Let's compare this to the relationship in holy marriage. Imagine what would happen if a spouse based quality time in marriage on how much he or she knew about his or her spouse. In such circumstances, it could be logically reasoned that quality time should diminish over the course of the marriage. What more is there to learn about someone you know so well? Why bother with constant quality time? Such thinking is ludicrous. Quality time is not based on amassing information.

God desires quality time with His people, not to coldly download information about Himself as if they were computers requiring bits of data. To "know God" in Scripture is never reduced to intellectual knowledge. The proper "knowing" of God is to find oneself in the place where God supremely expresses His love for His people. It is the place where faith is fed and nourished; it is the place where God protects us so that we are not overcome by the world; it is the place where His love causes us to love Him since He keeps pouring out upon His children the forgiveness of all their sins. This is why going to church can never be about just amassing knowledge. Luther wrote in the Large Catechism:

> Let me tell you this, even though you know God's Word perfectly and are already a master in all things: you are daily in the devil's kingdom [Colossians 1:13–14]. He ceases neither day nor night to sneak up on you and to kindle in your heart unbelief and wicked thoughts against [the Commandments of God]. . . . Therefore, you must always have God's Word in your heart, upon your lips, and in your ears. But where the heart is idle and the Word does not make a sound, the devil breaks in and has done the damage before we are aware [Matthew 13:24–30].[44]

If these things are clear in the mind of Christians, then they will understand why they must have the Word of God. To return to the analogy of holy marriage, at least one aspect of quality time includes a "knowing" that far surpasses the intellect, and the intimacy in marriage is something God uses to protect the couple from the temptations of the devil (1 Corinthians 7:5).

---

44   LC I 100.

Going to church is a way of renewing communion with God, and it is the way that Christians are preserved and protected in their faith. We know that this must be true since God has promised to send His Son through His Word and Sacraments. Why does Jesus come? He comes to save.

This realization also helps us to avoid the second bad reason for going to church: to perform a good work so as to check the box for what it means to be a Christian. Who could blame the congregant for thinking this way? After all, God commands His people to worship Him. That settles it, right? God would not command what He does not expect us to do. This is an easy transaction. Why shouldn't this be the reason for going to church? It is important that we don't misunderstand. Christians are certainly commanded to go to church, but this is not the only reason to go. If we turn church attendance into legalism, a great problem develops.

Treating church as a good work that makes us Christian is also a basic error, if not readily uncovered by theology, then certainly by logic. We do not want to be guilty of an absurd reduction. Jesus is recorded in St. Matthew's Gospel as quoting Isaiah the prophet: "This people honors Me with their lips, but their heart is far from Me" (Matthew 15:8). There is more behind going to church than trying to keep the Law of God. God wants more. He wants our hearts to be in it so that going to church isn't just about what we've "got" to do, but rather something we do eagerly because we "get" to do it.

The problem is that on our own, we can't give any more. In our sin, we do everything begrudgingly. This, however, is precisely why going to church is so important. Even if we drag ourselves to church only because we keep reminding ourselves of the commandment, even if we only go because of the commandment that subdues the sinful flesh trying to hold us back, what really counts is what happens after we get there.

While our motives may be astonishingly terrible, what the Lord does in return is grant us a feast of love and mercy once we get there. Many Christians testify to the feeling that even though they did not want to come, once they get there and receive God's gifts, they are so glad they did. This is a regular occurrence because of what the Divine Service (worship) truly is: when we try to make it about what we do, God comes along and reminds us that what makes church good is not our work but His. Going to church—engaging in worship—is, most importantly, the work of God. It is where God comes to serve us. Think of it: the Maker of heaven and earth, the King of kings, the Lord of lords, the Savior of the world, makes an appointment to meet up with us. He does it because He desires to give us His gifts of the forgiveness of sins, life, and salvation.

I was a brand-new pastor but feeling pretty confident about the excellent training I had coming out of seminary. I was attending one of the first fellowship events of my first congregation. I was twenty-five or twenty-six, and I sat down at a table with Vern, who was only about fifty years my senior. Vern was the congregation's treasurer. He and some other members were having a conversation about the significance of the numbers that reflect the life of a congregation, numbers like worship attendance and financial giving.

I arrived at the table and conversation to offer words of wisdom, and in this instance, a serious case of pietism. I interjected, "The holy ministry is not about numbers." My words hung in the air, and I could tell that my members were at least trying to show some respect to what their pastor had just uttered. Vern was gracious and humble, but he spoke up: "Well, Pastor, I disagree. I think that numbers often indicate where God's people are in their commitment to Him." I listened intently to Vern and realized that he had made a valid point. My words did not see the full picture, and while God's faithful people may be referred to as a "little flock" (Luke 12:32), Vern said something that was true. I had to admit as much to my people at that table. As for Vern and me, we ended up having a great relationship.

It was one of those nights when a pastor gets a call in the middle of it. It was Vern's daughter. I rushed to his house and got there as fast as I could. When I arrived, Vern had already died from a massive heart attack. The emergency personnel were placing his body in an ambulance, but his body was completely covered. I went into the house to see about Vern's beloved wife, Jane. She was in the living room, rocking back and forth, sobbing uncontrollably. Vern had had a heart attack and she had just lost the love of her life. They had been married for many decades. It was one of those moments when words were completely insufficient. All I could do was weep with the one weeping (Romans 12:15). I held Jane close and rocked with her, back and forth, on that couch. I held her for a long time. All of a sudden, Jane stopped rocking. She stopped, turned to look at me, and said, "Pastor, I am so glad that Vern was in church last Sunday to receive the Holy Sacrament!"

She was right, and in fact it had been an incredible thing for me to witness that Sunday in the Divine Service. I was standing up in the chancel, ready for the next group to come up for the Sacrament. In this particular sanctuary, communicants had to scale a few steps and then kneel at the rail. I had a chance to observe the considerable ordeal Vern had to endure. He could have waited for me and the elders to bring the Sacrament to him, but instead he insisted. He wanted to come up. His walking just to reach the bottom of the steps was labored, and then he required assistance to get up the steps. It was difficult for him to kneel. Everything was hard, and my heart went out to him.

Then the moment came when I got to serve this man of

faith the Blessed Sacrament, and the pain and discomfort on his face was completely gone. Replacing the agitation was the look of peace, the look of relief and comfort; the look of consolation was all that I saw on Vern's face. After the reception and blessing at the rail, he was happy. I was struck by this. Vern showed me where every Christian should want to be. It is where Christians belong.

THE LUTHERAN LENS—WHERE ARE WE?

UNCOVER INFORMATION

1. What are the *two kingdoms* every Christian lives in while alive on earth?

2. What are the first two ways that a Christian might respond in the public square?

3. In John 18:36, what does Jesus say about His kingdom? (In this context, the Lord refuses to merge or mix kingdoms, as "King of the Jews" [18:33] had political connotations.)

4. What might happen to the Church if it merged with the state?

5. Describe the two kinds of works done by the Christian and how they are *good* in their respective contexts.

DISCOVER MEANING

1. What are the basic differences between the two kingdoms on the one hand and the cultural designation of "church and state" on the other?

2. What is the difference between *special revelation* (what is in God's Word) and *natural law*, and how might these be used to testify in the public square?

3. The kingdom of power/government is *holy*. How is such a statement true and accurate?

4. Many Christians want to know how to live out their faith better in the world (at their jobs, etc.). How does properly understanding *vocation* help the Christian do this?

5. What are bad reasons to go to church? What is the right reason to go?

EXPLORE IMPLICATIONS

1. How would you respond to someone who says, "Christians should not bring their faith into the public square since matters of the state are not religious nor theological"?

2. In Matthew 5:13–14, the Lord Jesus refers to believers as salt to the earth and light to the world. What does living out this identity look like?

3. King Cyrus was a foreign king whose kingdom was associated with idolatry. And yet, he was used by God (consider again Isaiah 44:28). What does this say about how God can work through the state?

4. If a Christian is faithful in vocation, why should this enhance opportunities to share the Gospel?

5. What if the Christian doesn't feel like going to church? Why should they go anyway?

CHAPTER 10

THE LUTHERAN LENS—
WHEN ARE WE?

God's creation is still very good, and time is part of the creation. Therefore, time is very good. Time is a gift. The problem is what people do with it. Because of sin, people don't treat it very well. Christians are also guilty of this.

PRIORITY OF THE PRESENT

We have a habit of forgetting about the priority of being in the present, the only aspect of time that is immediately known and given. The psalmist wrote, "This is the day that the LORD has made; let us rejoice and be glad in it" (Psalm 118:24). The focus here is on the present day. We become wise when the present day is for us the most important day. It is the day given us to live in faith, hope, and love; it is a new day and opportunity to turn from sin and turn toward Christ. It is the day that testifies that God still has something for us to do on earth, whether we are to be as Christ as the one serving, or to be as Christ in being served (if He wills on a given day that we be "the least of these" [Matthew 25:40]), or both. Living in faith, the present day is a day for "fruitful labor" (Philippians 1:22). With this backdrop of today as the priority in time, St. Paul offers this counsel: "Look carefully then how you walk, not as unwise but as wise, making the best use of the time, because the days are evil" (Ephesians 5:15–16).

Because of sin, though, Christians lose track of the priority of the present. Instead we either slide into the past and potentially get stuck in it, or we get ahead of ourselves and start worrying about the future. Jesus once taught the first disciples, "Therefore do not be anxious about tomorrow, for tomorrow will be anxious for itself. Sufficient for the day is its own trouble" (Matthew 6:34).

THE CHRISTIAN VIEW OF THE FUTURE

This, however, doesn't mean we shouldn't think about the future. As a matter of fact, there is a different aspect of the future that we should not just be thinking about but yearning for. In other words, we have one exception to the rule about living in the present: when it comes to the glorious fulfillment of God's promises of heaven, the resurrection, and the new heaven and earth, Christians should have "eager expectation" (Philippians 1:20). St. Paul said that he strained forward "toward the goal for the prize of the upward call of God in Christ Jesus" (Philippians 3:14). In this respect, we should anticipate our death, knowing full well that there are marvelous things to come. The psalmist prayed, "So teach us to number our days that we may get a heart of wisdom" (Psalm 90:12).

PRESENT-FUTURE BALANCE: NOW AND NOT YET

We have, therefore, come to a balance. The Christian is to live in the *now* of their faith in Jesus Christ, but they are to also live in the *not yet* of what the Lord Jesus is going to do for them. Better said, Christians should live in the *not yet* of what is already theirs. Their glorious future is more than a guaranteed promise; it is a future that is *already* theirs since they are in Christ who is already risen and glorified. We say "not yet" only because we must wait to see the appearance of that glory. In the meantime, the Christian is both in the present time of faith in Christ and in possession of the future glory with Christ. This lens is the "now and not yet" of faith. It is the time of faith, the "when" of faith. This lens also helps the Christian see through a culture that is full of anxiety about the future.

Christians, of course, should think properly on the future. For example, Christians should be devoted stewards of the creation. It would be foolish to not plan for optimal care of the environment for our children and our children's children. Such a concern is an outgrowth of what it means to care for our families and communities. The problem is when any care about the future forsakes God, and oftentimes this comes with the presumption that man exists apart from the One in whom "we live and move and have our being" (Acts 17:28). When this happens, any preparation for the future is reminiscent of the tower of Babel, when mankind said, "Come, let us build ourselves a city and a tower with its top in the heavens, and let us make a name for ourselves" (Genesis 11:4).

SO-CALLED "CHRISTIAN" VIEWS OF THE FUTURE THAT RAISE ANXIETY

Sadly, even Christians get caught up in what easily becomes self-absorption in relation to the future. Self-absorption apart from God takes the kingdom of God as something not effected by God but effected by men and women. Simply put, people must get busy to guarantee that God's kingdom will finally arrive. Here, even Christians try to become the masters of their own destinies, and certainly to an extent, try to usher in a futuristic vision of the kingdom of God. This is heresy. It is also an old problem, and it began in the Garden of Eden when our first parents went along with the deception that they could top God and make His creation even better. That is, they got to the point of believing that they could be like God (Genesis 3:5). What God had given was no longer good enough. Even Christians get caught up in this discontent about the present that leads to some very problematic approaches to the future.

In the mid-1800s, John Nelson Darby systematized a theology that proposed several eras or epochs of time of how God relates to His people, something he called "dispensations." What is known as *dispensationalism* is often attributed to Darby, though he was certainly not the first Christian to propose that God works uniquely in various periods of time. Joachim of Fiore, for example, lived in the twelfth century, and he is famous for proposing that man's time on earth falls into one of three time periods, each one corresponding to one of the three persons of the Holy Trinity. It has been Darby's system, however, that has stayed around—particularly in the United States—in the twenty-first century.

These different time periods represent God using unique ways for saving people, an idea contrary to Scripture since the Old and New Testaments have the same Messiah-Christ, both teach being saved through faith in Him, and both rely on atonement through blood (the old covenant pointing to the blood of the Messiah). In dispensationalism, however, God's way of salvation is in flux. People were and are saved differently depending on when they find themselves living in human history. The current dispensation according to Darby's system is the "time of grace," or the Christian Church. It is the sixth dispensation with one more to go. The last or seventh one will be the so-called "millennial kingdom," a thousand-year period with Jesus ruling on planet earth.

Many have taken Darby's baton and run with it. C. I. Scofield published his famous study Bible at the beginning of the twentieth century, and this helped solidify dispensationalism in America. Other teachers have helped dispensationalism spread. In the 1970s, the single best-selling book in America (in any category) was *The Late, Great Planet Earth* by Hal Lindsey. In the 1990s and into the beginning of the twenty-first century, Tim LaHaye and Jerry Jenkins sold over seventy million copies of their *Left Behind* series. All these are examples of dispensationalism.

What this teaching has brought with it is anxiety about the future, the precise thing that Jesus said to avoid when it comes to the future (Matthew 6:34). That is, dispensationalism has latent in its teaching many additional, future-oriented ideas, such as what are claimed to be biblical prophecies of coming wars, the coming of the Antichrist, and the terrible—literalistic and inaccurate—fulfillment of the twenty-one judgments upon the planet as described in the Book of Revelation. Our purpose here, however, is not to get into these details (which demonstrate a complete departure from the proper interpretation of Scripture), but to bring out what all of this has in common: fear about the future and the incredible assumption that Christians must maneuver the future in the right way or face terrible consequences. With such a mentality, the coming of the Lord Jesus is not looked forward to with great comfort but with increasing anxiety.

Dispensationalism, of course, is not the only reason why people—including many Christians—live with so much anxiety, but so many of its popular themes have contributed to Christians living with fear toward the future. Popular Christianity in America has in many cases only made the situation worse. What are these reasons that interfere with understanding the "when" of our lives under God? What are these reasons that anxiety sprouts in the face of the future? More important, however, is the *answer* to these causes of anxieties. The answer comes through the right lens of faith that answers the question, when are we?

THE RIGHT VIEW OF THE KINGDOM
OF GOD AND THE POWER OF THE DEVIL

Two of the most important articles of the faith clarified by the lens of faith about time are the kingdom of God and the power of the devil. It is appropriate to discuss these side by side. We've already discussed the two kingdoms of power and grace—the left-hand kingdom and the right-hand kingdom— but now we are discussing the core meaning of "the kingdom of God." The kingdom of God is fundamentally about God ruling. Jesus Christ is King and where the King is, He rules. This rule of the Savior is the kingdom of God. Where Jesus is, the power of God is known.

After having cast out an evil spirit, Jesus was teaching about the kingdom of God in relationship to His authority over the demonic. He said, "But if it is by the finger of God that I cast out demons, then the kingdom of God has come upon you" (Luke 11:20). Corresponding to the exerting of Jesus' authority was the kingdom of God. Where Jesus is ruling, the devil no longer rules.

This is fantastically important. Many Christians have limited the kingdom of God to a future coming because of their insistence that at present, the devil must be freely reigning. "After all," they reason, "just look at all that is wrong in the world: substance abuse, sexual immorality, greed, lust for power, deception, and corruption. It must be that Satan is still in control." This, however, is precisely when a Christian is no longer walking by faith. In this case, God's hiddenness is unknown and the things of God are judged purely based on what is crassly observed. Similarly, when many witnessed Jesus dying on the cross, they saw nothing but satanic victory. What was hidden from their eyes, however, was the devil's decisive defeat.

The first Gospel promise recorded in Holy Scripture is

found in Genesis 3:15: "I will put enmity between you and the woman, and between your offspring and her offspring; He shall bruise your head, and you shall bruise His heel." God spoke to the serpent (a manifestation of the devil) in this prophetic word. The Lord's future orientation in this case was about a great confrontation that would result in the woman's offspring—a singular seed, a singular man—that would ultimately "bruise" the devil's head. *Bruising* occurs on both sides in this text, but one is applied to the head, the other to the heel. This difference is significant.

The strike to the head was a decisive one—one that led to the devil being defeated; the strike to the heel would cause an observable injury, and this corresponded to the Lord's death on the cross. We already know that the Lord's crucifixion cannot be construed as defeat, because three days later, Jesus conquered death. Even on the cross itself, however, Jesus was already defeating Satan's power by covering with His blood the sin that is the basis for the devil's accusation against God's people. On the cross, even as the Lord was dying, the devil's accusation was being silenced. The bruise against Christ was seen and grossly misinterpreted; the bruise against the devil wasn't even seen, and yet by it, the devil was being bound by God.

The devil is bound, but here dispensationalism tries to ruin the comfort of Christians. Because of its system that puts the so-called "millennial kingdom" as still future (the seventh dispensation), it interprets Revelation 20:2 on the binding of Satan as a future event. The truth, however, is that Revelation 20:2 records what has already happened. Already is the devil bound. Jesus' decisive victory on the cross guarantees it. It was for good reason that Jesus said at His dying breath, "It is finished" (John 19:30). What had to be done to the devil was done.

This truth is consistent with what Jesus had proclaimed about Himself after His resurrection from the dead: "All authority in heaven and on earth has been given to Me" (Matthew 28:18). The words aren't hard to understand. "All" means *all*. There isn't any authority left over for the devil. Still, even Christians can express frustration. "Why don't we see more evidences of Jesus' authority?" This again is the difference in how God's power is seen and known. Recall that Jesus said clearly, "My kingdom is not of this world" (John 18:36). He would not permit the purpose of His saving ministry to be confused with secular power. Nothing has changed. The Lord does not need to exert power over the economy or the trends on television to communicate the essence of His kingdom. Even if food and drink are not used rightly but are used to excess, "the kingdom of God is not a matter of eating and drinking," but rather, as the Scriptures say, "[about] righteousness and peace and joy in the Holy Spirit" (Romans 14:17).

However, what about Revelation 20:2? It says, "And [the angel] seized the dragon, that ancient serpent, who is the devil and Satan, and bound him for a thousand years." If the right view of time sees this as having already occurred, what about the thousand years? The Bible is in fact presenting a *millennium* of time. What do we do with this? The answer is straightforward. Revelation is uniquely written to deal with the Roman persecution at the time. St. John's language employed an apocalyptic genre full of what would otherwise be perceived as gibberish by those who would harm the underground Christian Church. St. John knew of this persecution as he wrote while in exile on the island of Patmos. His goal was to comfort the Christians on the victory of Jesus over all evil while using a literary genre bound by symbolism, figures of speech, and numerology as well as a cyclical and repetitive (reinforcing) language. Christians would be able to understand these themes since they were familiar with the Old Testament upon which the symbolism of Revelation is based. To them, the apostle's words were not gibberish.

The reason the number one thousand was used by St. John was to describe not a future period of time but rather the current and present time of the Christian Church. In Scripture, ten is the number of completion. For example, the Ten Commandments are a complete summary of God's Holy Law. This ten, however, is intensified here in Revelation. The complete kingdom of Christ is not just ten, but ten *cubed*. God is present in this completion even as He was present in the temple's Most Holy Place. This inner sanctuary was a perfect cube (1 Kings 6:20), and the future new heaven and earth is also a perfect cube (Revelation 21:16). Relationship to the Holy Trinity is possible. Be that as it may, the number one thousand takes on the character of perfect completion: it is the perfect time of Christ's perfect Bride "without spot or wrinkle . . . [but] holy and without blemish" (Ephesians 5:27). The biblical *millennium* is the time of Christ's Church and every individual member gathered around the Lord's Word and Sacraments.

Satan is bound during the Church's active ministry until the thousand years are ended and he is released for "a little while" (Revelation 20:3). In the meantime, he is completely bound. That means Satan cannot curtail the efficacy of the Word and Sacraments of Jesus Christ. The devil cannot stop sinners from becoming born again by water and the Spirit (John 3:5), and Satan cannot cancel the power of the Supper to forgive sins when it is received in faith (Matthew 26:28). In summary, Satan cannot stop the Church's holy ministry of converting sinners by the power of the Holy Spirit; and he can't stop the life of the Spirit that is brought into the world through the Word and Sacraments of Jesus Christ. Thus, Jesus said boldly and clearly, "The gates of hell shall not prevail against [My Church]" (Matthew 16:18).

In addition, even with all the problems in the world, the devil can't stop the life in the Spirit that belongs to Christians. Regardless of the world's darkness and persecutions, Christians still know the fruit of the Holy Spirit: "love, joy, peace, patience, kindness, goodness, faithfulness, gentleness, self-control" (Galatians 5:22–23). This new creation life (see 2 Corinthians 5:17) the devil can't cancel. So decisive is the victory of Christ over Satan that James can counsel Christians, "Submit yourselves therefore to God. Resist the devil, and he will flee from you" (James 4:7).

As for the darkness of sin that has remained in the world, why doesn't God eradicate it along with all the suffering it brings? If Jesus is indeed victorious, why not make the signs of His victory even clearer? Without trying to be redundant, the answer gets back to the Lord teaching that His kingdom is not of this world. Just as people once tried to make Jesus an earthly king, people are ready to make Jesus' kingdom an earthly one, confusing the significance of the saving Gospel itself. Indeed, if people make societal change the criterion for the power of the Gospel, then they will never be satisfied.

In truth, the way of God has never changed. Apart from His great miracles (though even these were criticized by some), Jesus just didn't tickle the fancy of many people. The popular idea is that during Jesus' public ministry, the number of His disciples only grew. This isn't true. In fact, because Jesus preached and taught the truth of His mission, He offended people left and right. The number of His disciples dwindled. After the Lord's great "bread of life" discourse recorded in the sixth chapter of John's Gospel, many were offended by His teaching. He said that His flesh was true food and that His blood was true drink, that He was the true bread from heaven, and that no one could come to Him unless it was granted by the Father. In the middle of the discourse, many of His disciples complained, "This is a hard saying; who can listen to it?" (John 6:60). Then when the Lord had finished His message, the Scriptures say, "After this many of His disciples turned back and no longer walked with Him" (v. 66).

Luther's Small Catechism teaches on the Second Petition of the Lord's Prayer, "Thy kingdom come." The question is asked in the catechism, "What does this mean?" "Answer: The kingdom of God comes indeed without our prayer, of itself. But we pray in this petition that it may come to us also." Then the question is asked, "How is this done?" "Answer: When our heavenly Father gives us His Holy Spirit, so that by His grace we believe His holy Word and lead a godly life here in time and there in eternity."[45] These words are extraordinarily helpful for our understanding of the kingdom of God.

We learn therefore that Christians have within themselves the rule of Christ. The kingdom of God is in their midst, but— and at the same time—the world itself does not change. In fact, if anything, the world is getting worse. This represents a conflicting situation to say the least: there is life in the Spirit that fills the Christian with light and spiritual vitality, but the darkness of the world is still hitting the Christian like a constant storm. This, too, is part of the "now" that the Christian knows. The Scriptures treat this tension as the norm. God therefore desires to encourage His people in the midst of the conflict. St. Peter wrote, "Beloved, do not be surprised at the fiery trial when it comes upon you to test you, as though something strange were happening to you" (1 Peter 4:12).

WHERE WE ARE AND *WHEN WE ARE* INTERTWINED: THE HOLY CROSS

Einstein demonstrated that space and time are inextrica-

---

45   SC III (The Lord's Prayer, Second Petition).

ble, not separate. We have come to an intersection ourselves about *where we are* (space) and *when we are* (time). Recall that a key focus of where we are is holy vocation. We have also confirmed that the "now" of when we are is characterized by conflict (and this is also consistent with chapter 7's *what we are*). The combination of this space and time is known as *the holy cross*.

The holy cross is whatever difficulties come with the faithful fulfillment of holy vocation. In the ceremony for holy matrimony, part of the traditional vows between the man and the woman are "for better, for worse; for richer, for poorer; in sickness and in health." The vows anticipate that while we go into holy marriage with joyful hope, we also commit to serving our spouse through the possibility of great suffering. Jesus said, "If anyone would come after Me, let him deny himself and take up his cross and follow Me" (Matthew 16:24). In following Christ is the taking up of a cross. The cross is a symbol of suffering and death. Suffering comes when we bear the burden of another, and at the very least the Christian must put to death that sinful tendency that only wants to live for self.

Such a life, however, is a tall order. How does anyone have the strength to do what we are now discussing? Bearing a cross comes about as naturally as cutting off a limb. Self-inflicted suffering isn't something we rush in to do. There must be a counter to this "now"; even if the "now" is marked by the quiet joy of the Spirit, it is nevertheless a "now" that needs help. No one knows this better than God does. That's why our time is not only "now," but also "not yet."

The "not yet" part of our time cannot just hang in the air as an idea. It isn't merely something we tell ourselves to make ourselves feel better. It isn't a mantra; it isn't psychobabble. Rather, the Lord has found a way for the "not yet" to enter our lives now. He does so by taking an aspect of the future and merging it with our present. This is not theoretical but actual. It is something that God has intended all along to do regularly and frequently in our lives. It is something God is still doing for His people today. For the Christian, the coming of Christ is not just an event in the future; it is an event that is also—at the same time—in the present, and it is something that we receive over and over again.

When my kids were growing up, I thoroughly enjoyed teaching them how to swim. Part of that was guiding them to get used to the water, and a big step was that first jump into the pool. What helped—tremendously, in fact—was that Dad was in the water already, waiting for them. I was there to catch them. They were guaranteed safety. Still, even with my calming voice and ready arms, that first time included extreme hesitancy. To this day, I smile as I see my children in my mind's eye, pacing back and forth along the edge of the pool, trying to muster courage to take that first leap. They wanted to do it, but, boy, was it hard. Once they did, though, and got past that initial shock of what it felt like to hit the water and begin to sub-merge, they would come up in my arms, and soon their wor-ried countenance was transformed into a smile. At that point, they wanted to do it again . . . and again and again and again. Before I knew it, they were pros.

ALWAYS READY FOR THE FUTURE THROUGH CHRIST'S CONSTANT COMING: HOLY COMMUNION

Similarly, if the coming of Christ is confined to one future event, then that singularity will be treated with the same sort of trepidation. We, too, will pace back and forth on the edge, treating what should raise exuberance in our souls as some-thing rather to fear. Too many Christians have treated the com-ing of the Lord as something that belongs strictly to the future, when it is something God has also given for our present. The

Lord brings the future to us today through His coming—His powerful and forgiving coming—in the Holy Sacrament of the Altar, also known as the Lord's Supper and Holy Communion.

The Ancient Christian Church never reduced the Holy Supper to a mere symbol. To the first Christians, it was what Jesus said it was. He referred to the bread as His body and He referred to the wine as His blood (Matthew 26:26, 28; Mark 14:22, 24; Luke 22:19–20; 1 Corinthians 11:24–25). A basic thought prevails here: since Jesus is the Word made flesh (God in the flesh), what He says must hold. While human reason and even imagination cannot grasp how something like this could ever happen, there is one thing that sustains the claim: "With God all things are possible" (Matthew 19:26). It is not unlike God speaking the creation into existence from nothing. God does what His Word speaks. For two millennia, the vast majority of Christians have held to the confession that Jesus truly comes—inexplicably and yet truly and powerfully—with the bread and wine in Holy Communion. In this way, Christians grow accustomed, in all holiness and sanctification, to receiving the Lord through His real coming constantly.

This is no small thing. This is the Lord of glory who comes to His people. The Holy Sacrament is so sacred that St. Paul warned that it is essential to recognize the body of Christ in the Sacrament so that it is not taken in judgment (1 Corinthians 11:29). This means that there is real preparation to be had in receiving this great gift, so that when Christians approach the altar, they meditate on the truth "Jesus died for me." On the one hand, this truth fills Christians with godly sorrow as they contemplate, "It was on account of *my* sin that Jesus died." This helps Christians remember the severity of their sin and their incredible need for the mercy of God. Then the contemplation continues: "Jesus died for me." Here, Christians are further reminded, "Jesus loves me—yes, me—so much that He willingly gave His life *for me*! Yes, *for me*! That is how much I am loved!"[46]

Then, the pastor approaches, lifts the Communion host before their eyes, and speaks the words "The body of Christ for you." At this precise moment as the body of Christ is given with the bread, God comes to the Christian in a special way. The Lord does not confine His presence with His people to only one kind of presence. For example, He promises to be with His people gathered together in His name (see Matthew 18:20). In the Sacrament of the Altar, however, Jesus is present through His real body and blood, the same that died on the cross, the same that rose from the grave, and the same that will come again in glory on the last day. Christians receive the risen Savior. Christians receive the body and blood of the Lord of glory—who has all power and authority in heaven and earth—in the very act of their eating and drinking.

FILLED WITH THE LIFE OF CHRIST EVEN NOW

This has distinct ramifications, and too often, many Christians aren't even aware of them. For one, in being filled with Christ, Christians become filled with life. Even the word *life* can be underestimated, because the life that Christ gives is eternal; it is so vital that it never ends. Imagine being given the opportunity to choose between two types of batteries: a regular battery that will last for months or a battery that will never die. Which one would you prefer? It is easy for people to treat biological life that ends to be all life, but they are unaware that there is another life, a life that is qualitatively different, a completely different kind of life. This life is the life of God Himself, and as a result, it is a life that can never suffer death. To receive Christ sacramentally is to be cemented into this second

---

46   Kurt Marquart, lecture at Concordia Theological Seminary, Fort Wayne, Indiana, ca. 1987–91.

life; it is to be truly filled with this life. As a result, when Christians die physically, they remain alive in Christ.

This means that the new life invades the old life. The old life still goes on its way. It is destined to die. It is temporary by nature, but the new life overcomes the old life so that the old life is no longer permitted to have the last word. When this life pervades, then the Christian—present tense—already crosses from death to life (John 5:24). Christians have in their present possession eternal life. This is an oft-neglected truth as too many Christians assume that eternal life begins after bodily death. No, eternal life—the "not yet" life that enables the dead to rise on the Last Day—is already given to the Christian. This life already lies within the Christian.

Within Christians who receive the risen Jesus resides the power of the resurrection. This means that now, the Christian's body that is perishable already has the imperishable residing in him or her; the dishonorable body—with all its weaknesses—already contains the glory and power of Christ (1 Corinthians 15:42–43). All of this, of course, is unseen. It is imperceptible. It is hidden. Nevertheless, it is also *there*. Job spoke confidently through the lens of faith: "For I know that my Redeemer lives, and at the last He will stand upon the earth. And after my skin has been thus destroyed, yet in my flesh I shall see God, whom I shall see for myself, and my eyes shall behold, and not another. My heart faints within me!" (Job 19:25–27).

This "not yet" life has an immense impact on the "now" life. Yes, we face many trials in the "now" life, but to be one in possession of the "not yet" life is to receive a dose of overwhelming perspective. The lens of faith leads us to see that our life, even now, is with God. With this great vision of faith, St. Paul said, "If God is for us, who can be against us?" (Romans 8:31). If the Christian knows that not even death can have the last word, what can any other problem do? Thus, Jesus said,

"Do not fear those who kill the body but cannot kill the soul. Rather fear him who can destroy both soul and body in hell" (Matthew 10:28). Ever wonder how the martyrs could be so bold in facing death? They were utterly convinced of the truth that they would never truly die.

Bringing this "not yet" life into the "now" changes everything. It doesn't matter what Christians must contend with. They are filled with the life of Christ. God is on their side. This does not mean that Christians live in reckless abandon, but it does mean that the future is not something to be feared. Instead, Christians have already seen it. Christ is there, and Christ is here. Now and not yet. This the lens of faith that can see. No clouds can hide it, so that Christians live in joy even under the weight of their crosses.

> Rejoice in the Lord always; again I will say, rejoice. Let your reasonableness be known to everyone. The Lord is at hand; do not be anxious about anything, but in everything by prayer and supplication with thanksgiving let your requests be made known to God. And the peace of God, which surpasses all understanding, will guard your hearts and your minds in Christ Jesus. (Philippians 4:4–7)

Bob is one of those amazing Christians—quiet, humble, but as steady and as generous as anyone could be. He loves God and he loves to serve and to share his faith. Just knowing and serving him strengthens me in my ministry. He has held up my arms as a friend and brother in Christ for many years. I am proud to be one of his pastors. He received a serious diagnosis, a form of cancer that has no cure. This disease, however, has quite simply failed to quell his spirit. He is a joyful Christian who continues to give of himself, giving to his family and giving to his church. By God's grace, Bob has epitomized what Garth Ludwig put forth so eloquently in his book *Order*

Restored.

The day Bob received his diagnosis, he called me and I shared something with him from Ludwig: there is a difference between the disease, the illness, and the sickness. Cancer was the disease, but it did not dictate Bob's reaction to it (his illness), nor did it mandate the way he had to be treated by others (his sickness). There is, in other words, a difference between the *objective phenomenon*, the *subjective, personal phenomenon*, and the *social phenomenon*.[47] Ludwig also taught that there is a difference between wellness and wholeness. Ludwig wrote, "This is why a distinction must be made between *wellness*, which means the ability to function, and *wholeness*, which means to live for a purpose."[48] Bob knows the "now and not yet." He is right with God. Consequently, the disease has not been permitted to unnecessarily make worse his illness or sickness. In the face of the disease, he has held on to his wholeness in Christ. He continues to live with purpose and with joy. Bob does this by the grace of God, fully confident of what the disease can never touch, his eternal life in Christ, a life that is already his.

---

47   Garth D. Ludwig, *Order Restored: A Biblical Interpretation of Health Medicine and Healing* (St. Louis: Concordia Publishing House, 1999), 31.

48   Ludwig, *Order Restored*, 128.

THE LUTHERAN LENS—WHEN ARE WE?

UNCOVER INFORMATION

1. Why should living in the present be the Christian's priority?

2. In what way should the Christian still think about the future?

3. What is the kingdom of God?

4. How much power and authority does the devil have today?

5. When does Christ come to the Christian today?

DISCOVER MEANING

1. How do Psalm 118:24 and Philippians 1:22 teach about how to live today?

2. Read Philippians 3:14. What precisely is the Christian's future focus?

3. If Christians are "in Christ" today (and they are), then what do we already know about our position in the future?

4. Genesis 3:15 teaches that Jesus would "bruise," or crush, the head of the devil. When was this prophecy fulfilled?

5. How much more meaningful is the Lord's Supper in terms of addressing any possible anxiety we have about the future?

EXPLORE IMPLICATIONS

1. Matthew 6:34 presents Jesus as warning specifically against anxiety about tomorrow. Describe why living in anxiety about the future opposes living in faith today.

2. Psalm 90:12 is not about morbidity and depression, but why is it so good for Christians to learn "to number [their] days?"

3. What terrible problems are raised if we insist that the kingdom of God is only future?

4. Someone says, "How can you say Jesus is reigning, with all of the ills and problems in the world?" What do you say in response?

5. If a Christian is trained in the constant coming of Christ, how will this Christian be helped regarding their preparation for Christ's great second coming?

CHAPTER 11

THE LUTHERAN LENS— WHAT DO I SAY?

THE LAW AND THE GOSPEL

What is real? What am I? To whom am I speaking? Where are we? When are we? There is one more duality, one more lens to consider, and, therefore, one more question: What do I say? The lens of faith regarding our speaking the faith boils down to two ways or two basic themes in Holy Scripture. One is called *the Law,* and the other is called *the Gospel. "Law and Gospel"* is a popular way for Lutheran Christians to speak, but in doing so they aren't being novel. St. Augustine, who lived well over a thousand years before Luther, wrote extensively of "law" and "grace"; same difference. There is no question that these are distinct themes in the Holy Bible. Both are from God, both are holy, both are necessary, and both are needed. At the same time, they are extraordinarily different in their message and serve completely different purposes.

The Law always focuses on the action or inaction of a person. It makes demands in the form of commands regarding what to do, and prohibitions regarding what not to do. The Law reveals the problem of sin, which by definition is the violation of the Law. "Sin is lawlessness" (1 John 3:4). It invariably describes the violation of God's Law in some way, shape, or form. In other words, God's Law reveals that we break the Law. An example of Law is the command to love God. As holy and good as this command is, the Law reveals that we fall short of it.

The Gospel always focuses on the action of God to save us through His Son, Jesus Christ. It makes no demands upon us whatsoever, but showers blessings upon us. It is a happy proclamation of what God freely gives us through Jesus. Jesus does all the work; we do none of it. Instead of giving commandments and prohibitions, the Gospel gives promises and assurances. While the Law is a great burden, the Gospel is a great relief. An example of Gospel is the proclamation that in Jesus Christ, God loves us apart from anything we are or anything we do.

Walther summarized the difference between Law and Gospel this way: "The Law issues only commands and demands. The Gospel, on the other hand, only offers. The Gospel does not take anything. It gives."[49]

MANY NOT AWARE OF THE DIFFERENCE

The problem is that many Christians are not aware of the distinction, and as a result, they painfully confuse God's Word. If the difference between Law and Gospel is unknown, then the Scriptures appear to be full of contradictions. If the difference, however, is known, then their relationship becomes elegant, exciting, and powerful. Once it becomes known that the Law is necessary to prepare for the Gospel, then what should be said to another person becomes as plain as day. Before people can be comforted by the sweet Gospel, they need to be convicted by the exposing Law. As the saying goes, therefore, "First things first." To change the order is disastrous.

---

49   Walther, *Law and Gospel*, 14.

I was excited about serving as a vicar in preparation for the pastoral ministry. (A vicar is like an intern, a seminarian serving in a congregation.) In my exuberance, however, I was pushing and straining myself, and before I knew it, a doctor was diagnosing me with bronchitis. As most people know, bronchitis, if not properly attended to, can quickly turn to pneumonia. However, I will never forget the doctor who helped me. Knowing what was going on, he sat down and gently spoke to me about the big picture. As I was in uniform, he knew that I was a Christian, and soon it became evident to me that he was a brother in Christ. He reminded me of the importance of taking care of my physical health precisely so that I could do God's work in the ministry. Then he prayed with me and asked God's blessing upon me. Talk about a doctor's appointment! Needless to say, he also treated me medically. First there was a diagnosis (joined with a loving admonition), and then came the medicine. There was an order to this. It was the only way I was going to get better.

However, the fact of the matter is that if people don't think they have a problem, then they will never be interested in a solution. God's Law is designed to be used by the Holy Spirit to convince people that they have a problem. The Scriptures say, "For by works of the law no human being will be justified in His sight, since through the law comes knowledge of sin" (Romans 3:20). St. Peter finished his great Pentecost sermon with these accusing and convicting words: "Let all the house of Israel therefore know for certain that God has made Him both Lord and Christ, this Jesus whom you crucified" (Acts 2:36). His last words were Law words. The Scriptures recorded the response that ensued: "Now when they heard this they were cut to the heart, and said to Peter and the rest of the apostles, 'Brothers, what shall we do?'" (Acts 2:37). It was only after St. Peter's convicting words, inspired by the Holy Spirit, that these listeners realized that they had a problem ("they were cut to the heart") and expressed concern for their situation ("what shall we do?").

Having said this, the Holy Scriptures also reveal that this is not the way a person will always respond to the Law. No one can manipulate or force a proper response to the Law, which is conviction and godly sorrow or regret over sin. No one can convince others that they need to confess their sin to God and seek God's help for their problem of sin. This is something that God Himself must do. Nevertheless, if God does it, He will do it through His people speaking the Law to others. This is the way God has promised to work as He has commissioned His Church to spread His message of Law and Gospel. In the meantime, Christians must wait on the Holy Spirit to work when and where He pleases to work in the hearts of people as only He can. This, by the way, does not contradict that God desires all people to be saved; but it reminds us that the timing for when faith comes is always in the hands of God. At the same time, we should never assume that because we trust in God's timing, we should be unconcerned about anyone who does not believe today. God warns, "Today, if you hear His voice, do not harden your hearts" (Hebrews 3:7–8, 15; 4:7). It is possible for a person to continue to resist God. It is possible for a person to die without knowing the benefits of the saving Gospel, the greatest tragedy.

MISUNDERSTANDINGS ABOUT THE LAW

Why would such resistance to the Law of God ever happen to begin with? There are many possible reasons, but two reasons are extraordinarily common: (1) many people assume that the purpose of the Law is not to reveal our sin problem, but instead, to serve as a standard to be met so that they would be rewarded by God; and (2) many others assume that the Law itself has been eliminated by the Gospel, so that the Law of

God is no longer applicable but has become superfluous and irrelevant. Many who call themselves "Christian" continue to hold to these false views.

The first wrong view is known as *legalism*. It is extraordinarily popular. Luther referred to this problem as "the presumption of righteousness," which he called "a huge and a horrible monster," which only the proper use of the Law can break.[50] It is a presumption because it is the natural assumption that people make about the Law. To the world, this is the natural form of religion as religion is equated with being good; if one is morally commendable, then he or she must be religious. While the assumption is popular, this sort of thinking has little to do with the Christian faith. In fact, true Christians confess that they are not good. Christians confess that they are sinners. Christians confess the truth of God's Word:

> For all have sinned and fall short of the glory of God.
> (Romans 3:23)

> For whoever keeps the whole law but fails in one point
> has become guilty of all of it. (James 2:10)

Christians confess that not only have they not attained the righteous standard of the Law but they have also actively fought against it. They say with St. Paul, "For I do not do the good I want, but the evil I do not want is what I keep on doing" (Romans 7:19). That is, not only do Christians not do good, they do evil. This is what the Law reveals. It is like a light to help us see that in fact, we have a huge problem as we stand before God who is perfectly holy. When the true situation soaks in, the Holy Spirit makes people alarmed. They start to sweat, so to speak, and realize that they need God's help, because no one else can help them. This is the purpose of God's Holy Law.

50   AE 26:310.

The idea that people can therefore use the Law to make themselves good and holy is biblically preposterous. There is a powerful scene in the Bible that brings this out. Once upon a time, a rich young man came to speak to Jesus about these matters, and he was completely convinced that this false view of the Law was the way to go:

> And behold, a man came up to Him, saying, "Teacher, what good deed must I do to have eternal life?" And He said to him, "Why do you ask Me about what is good? There is only one who is good. If you would enter life, keep the commandments." He said to Him, "Which ones?" And Jesus said, "You shall not murder, You shall not commit adultery, You shall not steal, You shall not bear false witness, Honor your father and mother, and, You shall love your neighbor as yourself." The young man said to Him, "All these I have kept. What do I still lack?" Jesus said to him, "If you would be perfect, go, sell what you possess and give to the poor, and you will have treasure in heaven; and come, follow Me." When the young man heard this he went away sorrowful, for he had great possessions. (Matthew 19:16–22)

LEGALISM CAN LEAD TO DELUSION

The rich young man was living in a state of delusion. He thought very highly of himself. The Law of God on which Jesus expounded was designed to remind the young man about God's convicting standard, beyond any ordinary person's ability to keep. God's true standard goes beyond mere external observance of the Law. Jesus also taught that the Fifth Commandment on murder is transgressed through hatred and cursing in the heart; and that the Sixth Commandment on sexual purity is also broken through lust in the heart (see Matthew 5:22, 28). For all these transgressions, the due penalty is death. "For the wages of sin is death" (Romans 6:23). This is the work of the Law. Its right use is to leave no doubt that one is under God's judgment. In love, God is alerting us to our problem so that we might receive (and desire) His solution.

The rich young man, however, was convinced that he was a great guy. He claimed that he had successfully kept God's Law, so Jesus, in great love, resorted to the one thing that would show the rich young man his sin. Jesus went to that one thing that would prove that he was a lawbreaker. The young man's money was something he loved more than God, but God has commanded, "You shall have no other gods before Me" (Exodus 20:3). The rich young man had broken God's Law. He loved money more than God. He knew it was true. This was why he walked away with sadness.

In this view, if we insist that the Law must be used to justify ourselves, the Gospel will continue to be resisted. If human pride insists on self-salvation through the keeping of the Law, then the Gospel might even make a person angry.[51] The idea that God would be the only one who can receive the credit for salvation is an affront to human pride, and it makes people resentful as they continue to reject the Gospel.

As self-salvation through keeping the Law is insisted upon, however, some unfortunate results occur (in addition to the main problem of rejecting the Gospel). One problem is that people can start to accept a delusional image of themselves. They can start to believe that they can keep—or have already kept—all of God's Law perfectly. The idea stems from a forced self-serving logic: "If God has given a commandment, then it must be that the commandment is capable of being kept." This is only partially true when a person is converted to saving faith, but it is never true apart from conversion by the Holy Spirit. It

---

51   Walther, *Law and Gospel*, 12.

is also never true that anyone can keep the Commandments perfectly, even among the converted. The unconverted may certainly perform good works in the civil realm, but none of their good works would be generated by faith since faith is absent. Bottom line: there is no way for people to justify themselves through good works. Keeping the Law can't save anyone because it is always being broken, even by Christians.

LEGALISM CAN LEAD TO DESPAIR

This problem of delusion is not the only issue that can arise from insisting upon the keeping of the Law. The other possible end result is utter and complete despair. When people become insistent that keeping the Law is the only way to please God and then they experience the reality of the situation, then talk about discouragement! In this case, they do not pretend to be good, nor are they successful in convincing themselves they are something they are not; instead, they see themselves in the mirror. That Law they are striving to keep just can't be kept, and they realize that they are failures in the face of their self-imposed project to keep the Law. The ramifications can be devastating. How can God accept them when the only way of being acceptable is impossible to attain? When despair happens, what often follows is giving up on the Christian faith entirely. Ironically, of course, what is here being assumed to be the Christian faith isn't the Christian faith at all. In the mind of the despairing, however, they might choose to leave anything that goes by the name of the saving faith. Talk about a catastrophe—and the only reason that any of this occurs is because of the wrong understanding about the purpose of the Law.

THE OTHER WRONG APPROACH: NO LAW AT ALL AND THE LOSS OF CONSCIENCE

This wrong way of viewing the Law, however, isn't the only significant misunderstanding out there. The other one goes to the opposite end of the spectrum: instead of believing that the Law must be kept, some people believe that the Law may be completely ignored. Theologians call this second major misunderstanding *antinomianism*. You can see within this fancy word the core similar to the Greek word *nomos*, which means "law." The word represents a position that says "anti-law-ism," as if to say, "There is no law." Some live as if the Law of God no longer exists. This happens in many forms, but in any form, it is extremely dangerous. If the Law is the only way of becoming aware of our sin problem and it is removed from life, then people will never become aware of their problem. The diagnosis of their sin, the real knowledge of their predicament, and most importantly, the knowledge of their need for God will be lost. This takes us back to the worst possible outcome.

The road traveled to come to this same end, however, is considerably different. To engage in denial of the Law is to automatically practice the rejection of conscience since God's Law is written upon the heart (Romans 2:15). Rejecting conscience, however, is to practice a lawlessness that deteriorates the soul. We work against ourselves. It is a like a spiritual autoimmune disorder. Self attacks self. This approach permits sin free rein with little or no resistance against the sin that is denied. It stops resisting that which is designed to destroy. The great irony here is that letting go of the Law is viewed as a *libertine* approach to living; nothing confines life anymore (theoretically). But by taking on this view, people enter a terrible prison. They are anything *but* free.

Libertinism that forsakes the Law makes a heart hardened by sin. The sin that is not seen, takes over as the conscience is lost. The spiritual predicament is described in Scripture when people strive to ignore what should otherwise be evident. It is like the prodigal son in Luke 15 who practiced reckless abandonment of all law. His moral degradation led to misery, and when he had exhausted all his resources, he was desperate for help (Luke 15:12–19).

This account in Scripture, though, has a good ending for the prodigal son. The prodigal son's misery led him to seek out his father, and he finally experienced unconditional love and mercy, but this is not always the outcome when conscience is rejected. St. Paul describes this alarming state of affairs in the Book of Romans:

> And since they did not see fit to acknowledge God, God gave them up to a debased mind to do what ought not to be done. They were filled with all manner of unrighteousness, evil, covetousness, malice. They are full of envy, murder, strife, deceit, maliciousness. They are gossips, slanderers, haters of God, insolent, haughty, boastful, inventors of evil, disobedient to parents, foolish, faithless, heartless, ruthless. Though they know God's righteous decree that those who practice such things deserve to die, they not only do them but give approval to those who practice them. (Romans 1:28–32)

What is described in Romans 1:28 as having been given up to a "debased mind" comes out similarly in 1 Timothy 4, especially as St. Paul describes the condition of "consciences . . . seared":

> Now the Spirit expressly says that in later times some will depart from the faith by devoting themselves to deceitful spirits and teachings of demons, through the insincerity of liars whose consciences are seared, who forbid marriage and require abstinence from foods that God created to be received with thanksgiving by those who believe and know the truth. (1 Timothy 4:1–3)

These are glaring warnings in the Word of God. They inform us that it is essentially possible that people can lose their sense of right and wrong. I am not trying to conjure thoughts of psychological pathologies, but rather I encourage you to see this through the lens of faith. There is a fundamental spiritual demise that occurs in the heart, which permits sin to reign. Sin eats at the conscience and eats at the soul. Furthermore, if people think they can soothe their conscience through "slight violations" or "outlets" that nevertheless compromise God's Law, then they only kid themselves. That situation is not unlike a person who tries to scratch less by scratching, or cough less by coughing. The more we sin, then the more we sin. The more God's Law is violated, the more the conscience deteriorates. If it happens enough, then the condition of "debased mind" and "seared conscience" will no longer be just a possibility.

THE DEBASED MIND DOES NOT MEAN ELECTION TO CONDEMNATION

The potential for this is mysterious. If all have sinned and fall short of the glory of God (Romans 3:23), how is it that some could potentially become so hardened when other sinners come to saving faith? The Lutheran Confessions address such questions:

> Whoever would be saved should not trouble or torment himself with thoughts about God's secret counsel, about whether he also is elected and ordained to eternal life. Miserable Satan usually attacks with these thoughts and afflicts godly hearts. But they should hear Christ, who is the Book of Life, and hear about God's eternal election to eternal life for all of His children.[52]

That is, biblical election is tethered to the Gospel and justification. Election is biblical, but it is only intended for those in

52   FC SD XI 70.

Christ. Election that gives certainty of salvation is intended for the Christian; it is not intended for speculating whether someone else is going to hell. There is no "double election"; God elects no one to hell, because Jesus Christ has died and risen for all.

Still, the question for a given individual is whether he or she will continue to resist the Holy Spirit. Jesus once looked over Jerusalem during His public ministry and bemoaned: "O Jerusalem, Jerusalem, the city that kills the prophets and stones those who are sent to it! How often would I have gathered your children together as a hen gathers her brood under her wings, and you were not willing!" (Matthew 23:37). The Savior was pushed away. All of this is to say that to ignore the Law is to lose conviction of sin, and to lose conviction of sin is to lose the possibility of finally seeing that one needs the Gospel.

The Christian therefore must be aware of these two other interpretations of the Law of God. Even if a Christian knows that someone else needs the Law in order to see their sin, the Christian must also be cognizant of the possibility that the non-Christian may assume that the Law itself is the way to salvation (and must be kept) or that the Law is now passé (and should be held as inconsequential). These two possibilities, however, do not cancel the clear need for the Law and, of course, its proper usage. Walther said, "As long as people are at ease in their sins, as long as they are unwilling to quit some particular sin—in this situation you must preach only the Law, which curses and condemns them."[53] Walther also said, "as long as the devil still keeps [someone] in bondage with even one **individual** sin, [then they] are not yet a proper object upon which the Gospel can operate."[54] People must be convinced that their sin is a mortal problem. If not, then sin will envelope them either to deception, despair, or degradation.

---

53   Walther, *Law and Gospel*, 22.
54   Walther, *Law and Gospel*, 22.

WHEN TO SHARE THE LAW

So how is the Law shared? The moment a Christian knows that another person with whom they are interacting is, as Walther says, "at ease in their sin," then that person should be warned. This is never done in a way that assumes an air of superiority. Remember that 1 Peter 3:15 speaks of the faith shared with "gentleness and respect," gentleness toward the one spoken to and respect to the Lord, who is listening. That is, we share the word of Law driven by love and the overwhelming conviction that the one with whom we are speaking is worthy of the blood of Jesus Christ shed for the world. This one fact supplies all the motivation we need and assures us that our sharing is extraordinarily worthwhile.

With this in place, how does the Christian priest share the Law with gentleness? A natural way of achieving gentleness is to remind oneself that one is also a sinner. Christians have just as much need for the ministry of Law and Gospel as anyone to whom they are speaking. Christians should strive to put themselves in the same boat, because they are. Without the constant application of God's Law, Christians would lose their faith. Then they would no longer thirst for the Gospel that keeps their faith living and active.

Christians therefore are not sharing the Law they've already conquered, or the Law they've graduated from, but rather they are sharing what they themselves know they need. In fact, this last point doesn't go far enough. The truth is that because Christians see and know their own sin, then they ought to be able to relate to St. Paul, who considered himself the worst of sinners (1 Timothy 1:15). This means that it should be practically impossible to ever talk down to someone. It should be out of the question for the Christian to adapt an air of superiority. The Christian can be gentle because the Christian knows genuine humility.

To arrive at humility, however, is also to arrive at the fact that the humble one does not reflect on his or her humility. Humble people do not bow their head to thank God for their deep humility. As a matter of fact, if humility is ever achieved, then it is because the Law is doing what God intends for it to do. If humility is achieved, then the person is quite positive that he or she is not humble. With this attitude, however, we are in a good position to speak to those without Christ. With this attitude, we know that there is no way whatsoever that we are any better than they are. If this does not inspire gentleness, nothing will.

WHEN TO SHARE THE GOSPEL

What happens, however, when people come to the point of realizing their sin problem? Then the Christian must transition from communicating the Law to speaking the Gospel. When this happens, there is a seismic shift, from focusing on the action of the people to the action of God. No more do Christians speak about any failure of those to whom they are speaking. Rather, Christians convey only that this person is now the recipient of the greatest blessings that can possibly be described. Gospel takes over because one is no longer secure in his or her sins, but rather is frightened.[55] Then the person is ready to hear the Good News so that through faith in it, God would chase fear away and make the person new. These are two of the major effects of this Gospel clearly stated:

1. In the first place, while the Gospel demands faith, at the same time it also offers and gives us faith.

---

55   Walther, *Law and Gospel*, 22.

2. [In the second place] the Gospel . . . takes all terror, all fear, all anguish from them, filling them with peace and joy in the Holy Spirit.[56]

These two effects should be understood. The first effect reminds us that for the Gospel to be personally beneficial, then faith is completely necessary. This necessity, however, is often presented in ways that confuse Law with Gospel. When this occurs, faith is treated not as God's creation but as man's decision.

THE GOSPEL—NOT HUMAN WILL—GIVES FAITH

Some falsely present faith as something a person must generate for the Gospel to be effective. This is the idea that God has done His part (He has taken the way to salvation as far as He can take it), but now one thing is still needed (recall the one thing needed in Luke 10:42 that isn't faith): we must do our part. God is reaching down, but we must reach up. God is calling, but we must believe. At the end of the day, it all comes back down to us. God is waiting, if we would only finally let Him in. Faith in this case comes because of our monumental achievement; it becomes the greatest single work a person could ever do. When Christians treat faith this way, Law replaces Gospel. Such an approach has Christians acting as if they have climbed a mountain that others haven't and reserve the right to look down on those still climbing. This is *not* how the Scriptures approach faith.

When this happens, however, then what is purely free (the Gospel) becomes something diluted and no longer free. The Gospel becomes hinged to a gigantic requirement: namely, what some call "faith." Giving this impression puts everything back on those hearing the message. In other words, they have been led back to what they must do. They are back to the Law.

---

56   Walther, *Law and Gospel*, 20.

If they fail to form faith in themselves, then game over. Such thinking destroys the presentation of the Gospel.

Yet, many Christians feel justified in this position. What might be the most widely used Scripture to support this idea is Revelation 3:20: "Behold, I stand at the door and knock. If anyone hears My voice and opens the door, I will come in to him and eat with him, and he with Me." For those who treat faith as coming from people, this Scripture seems irrefutable. Jesus comes to the person, but the person must then let Jesus into his or her life. What could possibly be clearer? The problem, however, comes when we see that such an interpretation misses the fact that Jesus in Revelation 3 is speaking to the Church in Laodicea. However, the Church, by definition, is composed of Christians with faith. That is, Jesus here is not telling people to form faith in themselves; He is describing a response when faith is already had. Revelation 3:20, therefore, cannot be treated as initiating the relationship between God and the sinner by faith.

As a matter of fact, in describing how people first come to God (which always requires faith), the exact opposite is true. People do not enable themselves to come to God, but God enables them. God is 100 percent responsible for the formation of faith and is thus completely responsible for the birth of faith within those coming to God. In John 6:37, 39, Jesus clearly taught that the Father is the one who gives people to His Son. Read these two verses and ask, "According to these Scriptures, how does one come to Christ?" Answer: "By the Father who gives them." Jesus continues this teaching in verse 44: "No one can come to Me unless the Father who sent Me draws him." Ask again, "According to this verse, how does one come to Christ?" Answer: "By the Father who draws him." The teaching is no less clear verse 65: "And He said, 'This is why I told you that no one can come to Me unless it is granted him by the Father.'" How does one come to Jesus? According to this Scripture, the Father must grant it. In all these Scriptures, who is responsible for anyone coming to Christ? It is not the person. It is God.

This teaching is also consistent with John 15:16, where Jesus taught His first disciples, "You did not choose Me, but I chose you." If *anyone* "decides" on conversion by faith, it is God. The teaching presented here in the New Testament is totally consistent with the Old Testament. In Ezekiel, the Lord describes what He will do for His people in leading them back to the Promised Land:

> I will sprinkle clean water on you, and you shall be clean from all your uncleannesses, and from all your idols I will cleanse you. And I will give you a new heart, and a new spirit I will put within you. And I will remove the heart of stone from your flesh and give you a heart of flesh. And I will put My Spirit within you, and cause you to walk in My statutes and be careful to obey My rules. (Ezekiel 36:25–27)

The revelation from Ezekiel is nothing short of remarkable. The Israelites could take zero credit for their life of faith. Their new heart came from God. Their holy movements and life were from God. Everything about their faith was from God. This confirms the truth: faith is a gift. Faith is indeed completely necessary, but it is not our doing. It is God's. Walther's elaboration here is priceless:

> What if someone says, "But the Gospel demands faith!" Well, just picture someone who is hungry. You tell him: "Come, sit down at my table and eat." That hungry person would hardly reply, "Who are *you* to boss me around?" No, he would understand and accept your words as a kind invitation. That is exactly what the Gos-

pel is—a kind invitation to partake of heavenly blessings. . . . The Law issues only commands and demands.
The Gospel, on the other hand, only offers. The Gospel
does not take anything. It gives.[57]

Walther elaborated further by quoting Luther:

In offering us help and salvation as a gift and donation
of God, the Gospel bids us to hold the sack open and
have something given to us. The Law, however, gives
nothing. It only takes and demands things from us.
Now, these two, giving and taking, are surely far apart.
For when something is given to me, I am not contribut-
ing anything toward that. I only receive and take, I have
something given to me.[58]

The call to believe, therefore, describes the Gospel as
"free" and "for you," so that the focus is not about our doing in
order to get, but getting while the receiving is inevitable. It is
the gift, then, that is emphasized. The gift is so great, so priceless, so glorious, so attractive, so relieving, that we uncon-
sciously gravitate toward it and we find ourselves receiving
it with hungry hearts. In this case, we are far less concerned
with our action and are infinitely more preoccupied with what
is being received.

Think of small children mesmerized by a bright, shiny
Christmas present. They hold it, unwrap it, and open it, but
they are practically unaware of these actions. All that matters
is the gift itself. The gift of Christ's Word itself creates faith. It
is knowing that Jesus is the answer to one's great burdens;
that He has come to remove guilt and shame; and that He
has opened heaven to us. Through His gift of Himself to us,
our life on earth has meaning. When we see this through the
lens of faith, then we are like the woman in Luke 7 who could

---

57   Walther, *Law and Gospel*, 14.
58   Walther, *Law and Gospel*, 23–24.

only adore Jesus with her tears of joy. The Word of God tells us where faith comes from. It is not from grinding our teeth and clenching our fists. Romans 10:17 puts it this way: "So faith comes from hearing, and hearing through the word of Christ." Faith comes from the outside, not the inside. Faith comes from Jesus and His Word, not from our hearts. While faith finds itself in our hearts, it does not originate there.

My firstborn was still very young, only two and a half years old. He had been baptized and already had faith, but I was reminded of how the Word from the outside not only generates this faith but also excites it and feeds it. *Extra nos*, Latin for "outside of us"—this is where our salvation and strengthening come from. I saw this again with my little boy. My wife and I were sitting on our apartment sofa, watching the Christmas story on television. The scene of the birth of Christ was about to come on. The movie started with the star of Bethlehem and then panned down to the stable, where a tiny baby was being born beyond the animals blocking a full view. Then the baby started to cry and the message from the angels began to be celebrated: "A Savior is born!" I called to my little son, "Come, come, hurry, and see!" He ran to my side and watched all of this with wide eyes. As the scene climaxed with the birth of Jesus, he wanted to get something out but couldn't. He was overwhelmed with emotion and excitement. His little body started to shake. Tears of joy began to roll down his cheeks. As he could not contain himself, he started running in place. I sat there, stunned. I was witnessing the message of the birth of the Savior come upon my little boy. I saw what it did to him, and as a result, faith illuminated him. I will never forget this scene as long as I live. He grew up to become a pastor. God had created faith in him and caused his faith to spill over. Through all of this, the Gospel was the focus.

When the Christian shares the Gospel to the hungry soul that feels its need for the Gospel and has let go of resistance, then the focus is on the Gospel proper: what Jesus has done for the sinner. The Christian shares the gifts of the forgiveness of sins, life, and salvation won, and the burdens of sin, death, and the power of the devil are conquered. The Gospel proclaims what we are saved *to* and what we are saved *from*. Jesus has accomplished all the work. He has delivered from the bad and to the good. It is all gift. When this is the preoccupation and emphasis, then when the Christian says, "Believe!" it is like the starving person is presented with a feast and hears "Eat!" All the person sees is the gifts of food. The believing, the *eating* that is faith in the Gospel, only cares about the Gospel. The believing takes care of itself.

THE GOSPEL REPLACES FEAR WITH PEACE AND JOY

This leads us to the second effect of the Gospel. As long as people believe that the only way to peace is that they must perform, then they will never know whether they've performed enough. In this case, a great burden remains. With the Gospel, though, the demand for performance is eliminated and there is only relief. Love overcomes fear. God's Word says, "There is no fear in love, but perfect love casts out fear. For fear has to do with punishment, and whoever fears has not been perfected in love" (1 John 4:18). When the Holy Spirit births faith and takes all terror, fear, and anguish away, He doesn't stop there. Recall that the Gospel not only delivers *from* but delivers *to*. It is important for the Christian to know that the Lord not only grants release from fear and relief from a great burden, but He also grants a new life of peace and joy. The Holy Spirit liberates from the old way and gives a new way that includes His virtues. That is, He puts us into Jesus Christ, and to be in Christ is to know His life. The life of Christ exudes peace and joy.

Peace and joy in Christ are easily misconstrued. Some people think they have discovered a great disharmony in the Bible. On the one hand, Jesus is called the "Prince of Peace" (Isaiah 9:6), and when He was born, the angels proclaimed: "Glory to God in the highest, and on earth peace among those with whom He is pleased!" (Luke 2:14). On the other hand, Christ Himself taught His first disciples (and us): "Do not think that I have come to bring peace to the earth. I have not come to bring peace, but a sword" (Matthew 10:34). Let us therefore be clear: the Bible teaches that Jesus Christ has come to bring peace, and the Bible teaches that Christ has come not to bring peace.

No, this isn't one of those so-called contradictions that skeptics like to assert. Rather, the Holy Scriptures put before us two different forms of peace. One kind of peace is the cessation of hostility between people in the world. The Scriptures have never promised this outside of heaven and the new heaven and earth that comes after the resurrection. Even when the Old Testament predicted the birth of Christ as Prince of Peace, it also predicted His own Passion on the cross of Calvary (Psalm 22). Jesus Himself guaranteed that His disciples would also suffer: "If they persecuted Me, they will also persecute you" (John 15:20). As a matter of fact, the Lord Jesus helped to teach about the tension when He put the two opposite ideas side by side:

> Blessed are those who are persecuted for righteousness' sake, for theirs is the kingdom of heaven. Blessed are you when others revile you and persecute you and utter all kinds of evil against you falsely on My account. Rejoice and be glad, for your reward is great in heaven, for so they persecuted the prophets who were before you (Matthew 5:10–12).

TWO KINDS OF PEACE AND JOY:
HORIZONTAL AND VERTICAL

Jesus clearly taught His disciples to anticipate not peace from people but persecution from people. Yet, by virtue of belonging to the Prince of Peace, these same disciples could rejoice and be glad. This informs us about a different kind of peace. Whereas the cessation of hostility between people might be described as a *horizontal peace*, the peace that God gives may be properly known as a *vertical peace*. The peace that Christ gives is peace with God. This peace knows that regardless of whatever happens on earth, God is now on our side to always love us and to continue to bless us. This is where the prior consideration of what is real—the seen and unseen, the theology of glory versus the theology of the cross—become very important to remember.

To have Jesus' peace is no promise from God that life will be easy or that we will suddenly have rest from the world. Not at all. In respect to the ongoing conflict from the outside (chapter 1) and from the inside (chapter 2)—especially in light of our conflict and battle from within (chapter 7)—the Christian continues to know a real lack of peace. Walther is up front about this:

> Again, if you were to portray Christians as exceedingly happy people—completely without worry or trouble of any kind—once again, you would not be painting a true picture. In reality, Christians suffer from far greater anxiety, worry, and tribulation than do worldly people.[59]

At the same time, Walther goes on to teach the other side:

> Yet, despite all this, Christians are far happier than worldly people. If God were to come to them that very

59   Walther, *Law and Gospel,* 61.

night and demand their souls from them, they would say, "Praise God! My race is run; I will soon be with my Savior." On the other hand, amid their tribulations they think: "Surely, it will not be long before I can go home to my Father in heaven, and all the misery and woe of this earth will be long gone and forgotten."[60]

Peace with God is the absolute assurance that we are 100 percent secure in life. Christians enter into the realization that with God on their side, they are in a perpetual win-win throughout life. St. Paul described this new state of assurance this way:

> For to me to live is Christ, and to die is gain. If I am to live in the flesh, that means fruitful labor for me. Yet which I shall choose I cannot tell. I am hard pressed between the two. My desire is to depart and be with Christ, for that is far better. But to remain in the flesh is more necessary on your account. (Philippians 1:21–24)

Do you see the win-win? Knowing the peace of Christ in his life, St. Paul knew that he was completely covered by good. If he died, then he got to be with Christ, and this was the best possibility. If, however, he was to remain on earth, then it meant "fruitful labor," a productive life for God to work through, especially through holy vocation. All that is the Lord's is already given, and all that we do now is blessed with His ongoing presence. The "now and not yet" guarantees the win-win. These are the reasons the Christian knows peace even now in this life.

The Christian also knows joy. How is this reconciled when the Christian also knows anxiety, worry, and tribulation? Again, the difference between the horizontal and the vertical is very important to keep in mind. There are many things in the world that cause Christians pain. Christians continue to mourn (Mat-

---

60   Walther, *Law and Gospel*, 61.

thew 5:4); they continue to hunger and thirst for righteousness (Matthew 5:6); and as we've already mentioned, they continue to be persecuted. This means that very often they feel the opposite of joy. Sadness is familiar to Christians.

This sadness, however, leads them to call on the Lord, and in being brought to Jesus again and again, the rest of the story is known. When Christians find themselves in need, the Lord in grace leads them to His help. Then the realization settles in that Jesus is keeping His promises no matter what is faced: "No one will snatch them out of My hand" (John 10:28). He is standing by His guarantee: "I will never leave you nor forsake you" (Hebrews 13:5). Then Christians know that with God unconditionally on their side, that even what makes us sad in the world is worked for good (see Romans 8:28).

This Gospel is easy to share as it is completely preoccupied with the benefits for the people being spoken to. Imagine that. All we are doing here is expressing the unceasing gifts of God in Christ to them. It is a fact: they are loved on account of Jesus. It is beyond doubt: they are forgiven through Jesus. It is indisputable: they have eternal life in Jesus. It is certain: God is on their side in Jesus. They, too, can have this confidence: "If God is for us, who can be against us?" (Romans 8:31). These things bring joy, a joy that is known no matter what is faced. This joy is the quiet conviction that one is safe; that one will be blessed regardless of the externals in life; it is the relief of knowing that life works out for good and that nothing can remove our greatest blessings. They are in place. Even what the world considers to be the worst disruptions, even these cannot remove what is already given in Christ. In this Christians know joy. The joy of the world is fleeting. It comes and goes based on fluctuating circumstances, but the joy of the Christian is constant. It never leaves, because the gifts of God in Christ are always known.

KEEPING JOY OVER SADNESS:
INDIVIDUAL CONFESSION AND ABSOLUTION

Patty was one of those parishioners who permitted me to serve her one-on-one. Most people do not realize the enormity of the blessing granted the pastor when this happens in holy ministry. When pastors are permitted to personally encourage and equip God's people with the Word of Christ, then their call is celebrated and reinforced. This is good for the pastor. It reminds him of what is truly important in the holy ministry: always giving the Word of Jesus, and always giving His Sacraments. Patty came hungry and thirsty. She was suffering.

I was just starting out in the ministry. I was eager to serve, and as I mentioned before, I felt good about the training I had received at an excellent seminary, but I was quite simply intimidated by what Patty brought to me. She was very depressed. The word *depression* is thrown around a lot, and we must be careful in our use of the word. Patty had been professionally diagnosed with depression. The pastor in such a case is to remind himself of God's many resources and not try to do what he is not trained to do. Pastors aren't psychotherapists and should not pretend that they are.

God in His love and mercy has given good doctors to consider the chemistry of depression, and good therapists to treat the psychology of depression. Good nutritionists and other professionals are also equipped to direct the whole person to better cope with depression. What Patty brought to me, though, was a depression that was already being treated. She was already being a good steward of God's resources. She knew the benefits of counseling, a good twelve-step program, and medication. Still, she was heavy laden, and what she was enduring was exhausting her.

She felt instinctively that there was still something else

out there. She felt compelled to come to her new pastor and bare her soul, seeking yet another way to help her under her great load and her sharp pain. As she explained the details, I was frankly feeling a mounting sense that what she was going through was beyond my pay grade to help. Patty and her husband had been blessed with a son whom they loved very much, but then they were also blessed with a daughter. Her name was Brenda. One nightmarish day, however, Brenda died. They call it sudden infant death syndrome. In the middle of their loving and meticulous care, their baby girl left this world. The love of their life was gone.

As painful as this was, however, a new pain came with Patty's realization that no matter what she did to try to make things better, everything seemed to be getting worse. She was starting to feel as though everyone was giving her something more to do. In time, she was overwhelmed with tiredness. Nothing was working for her. She was starting to feel desperate. Life was living in a cell of pain and frustration. With all this came a profound sadness. She wanted to serve. As a Christian, she wanted to serve God and His Church, but she felt she didn't know how. In the meantime, her body was more sluggish, her hope to get pregnant again was frustrated, tensions in relationships were mounting, and the sense of aimlessness was becoming familiar. This was the way our relationship started, and I felt inept. What could I do to help my dear sister in Christ?

Intellectually, I knew even during our first meeting that there was nothing I could do to help Patty. There was nothing I could say or tell her to do. Little platitudes would not help. Heaping a spiritual program on her, telling her to pray more and read Scripture more, would be to mount Law prescriptions upon her conscience that could very well push her over the edge.

With the Holy Spirit leading, I told her about what I could

not do, but then we started to speak about what God does. I had been taught about the wonderful gift given our Church that was now falling into disuse. It needed to be rediscovered and offered again. It was time to take it out of the closet, dust it off, and see its brilliance again. I shared with my sister in Christ about the gift of individual Confession and Absolution. This was not to replace the important resources already hers. I did not tell her to stop attending the support group or to rule out her counselor or doctor. I simply focused on what the Lord does through this gift that specializes in Christ lifting our burden and replacing it with His absolution. Patty was invited to confess her great burden to the Lord. In response to our confession, the comfort of the Gospel is given to us over and over again. Luther knew about the gift:

> If you were a Christian, then you ought to be happy to run more than a hundred miles to Confession and not let yourself be urged to come. . . . When I urge you to go to Confession, I am doing nothing else than urging you to be a Christian. . . . For those who really desire to be true Christians, to be rid of their sins, and to have a cheerful conscience already possess the true hunger and thirst. They reach for the bread, just as Psalm 42:1 says of a hunted deer, burning in the heat with thirst, "As a deer pants for flowing streams, so pants my soul for You, O God." In other words, as a deer with anxious and trembling eagerness strains toward a fresh, flowing stream, so I yearn anxiously and tremblingly for God's Word, Absolution, the Sacrament, and so forth. . . . Let us, however, lift our hands in praise and thanksgiving to God [1 Timothy 2:8] for having graciously brought us to this our understanding of Confession.[61]

We set up our next meeting. The goal was clear: it was not

---

61   BEC 30–35.

for me to give her stuff to do, but to give her what God had done for her because she was loved. The gift of absolution was hers. She was baptized. All the kingdom gifts were hers. It was time for us to simply receive them more often and rest in them. We didn't wait long to get started. Some think that this gift should not treat the same sin, but this is a gross misunderstanding of the gift. It's true that God forgets our sins (Isaiah 43:25; Hebrews 8:12), but we aren't Him. We tend to remember them and we struggle to keep them buried. No one knows this better than the Lord does. No one. He also says, therefore, "I do not say to you seven times, but seventy-seven times" (Matthew 18:22). While we may struggle to keep those sins buried, God knows how to bury them. His Word does it, so He never tires of forgiveness. I mention this because the pastor should never say, "Okay, I'll give you three sessions, and then we're done." Pastors who are undershepherds walk with their sheep. They live with them. This living can never be reduced to a few meetings or sessions.

None of this is to say that I didn't have my doubts about what we embarked on, because given the severity of Patty's cross, I agreed to see her once per week and of course to be on call in between. Needless to say, we also spoke of the necessity of faithfulness in attending Divine Service and the priority of receiving the Holy Supper. Still, the time commitment was considerable, the emotional investment not an easy thing, and I would need patience. I had to call on the Lord to help and to provide. That was the only way any of this was going to happen.

We started and we kept meeting for years, and as I look back, I have to say that what ensued has been nothing short of amazing. In fact, I don't have the words to describe it. Patty still bears her crosses, she still has problems, and she still feels her sin—in fact, probably more than ever before—but something else has happened. The sense of the tiredness of seeking help in the world has left her. She has been given an incredible faith to rejoice in the help that God gives her 24/7. She can have those moments of melancholy still, but the depression is nothing like it was. I won't mention specifically which of the other resources she simply no longer needed, but I will say that many of them she stopped. The Lord had worked a great work, and His Gospel in the absolution had been and continues to be powerful.

Her life changed. I don't know how else to say it. She laughs more than she used to. She has become bold—not obnoxious, but joyfully open for Christ and His Gospel. She serves with a glad heart. She yearns for the Word and Sacrament. Her womb was opened and God gave her and her husband another son, and he has become—like his older brother—another great joy in their lives. Furthermore, Patty became a deaconess in the Church and served for many years, sharing the Word and gladly bearing the burdens of others. In my opinion, she has become a depiction of what it means to not only know what a Christian is delivered from, but also what a Christian is delivered to. She also knows peace and joy.

How does she share the Gospel? She is compassionate. She listens to people and applies St. Paul's principle of becoming all things to all men (1 Corinthians 9:22), that is, getting into their shoes and lives through sincere interest and care for the other person. She serves unconditionally and lets people see her love for them, and she looks for those opportunities to say that God loves and forgives that person she is serving. She can tell them that this is completely certain and true, because of what Jesus Christ has done.

The Christian knows the effects of both the Law and the Gospel. Walther explained:

Like two hostile forces, Law and Gospel sometimes clash with each other in a person's conscience. The Gospel says to you, "You have been received into God's grace," while the Law says to you, "Do not believe it. Just look at your past life. How many and how serious are your sins! Examine the lustful thoughts and desires that you have harbored in your mind." On occasions such as this it is difficult to distinguish Law and Gospel. When this happens to you, you must say, "Away with you, Law! All your demands have been fully met, and you have nothing to demand of me. There is One who has already paid my debt."[62]

In seeing through the culture that does not know what to say to find peace in this life, the lens of faith sees and knows exactly what to say. The answer is to speak the Law and to speak the Gospel. These not only guide us, but they keep us alive in Christ.

---

62   Walther, *Law and Gospel,* 53.

THE LUTHERAN LENS—WHAT DO I SAY?

Uncover Information

1. What are the two basic ways or themes of God's Word?

2. How would you describe the two common misunderstandings about the Law of God?

3. When should a Christian share the Law with someone? When should a Christian share the Gospel with someone?

4. What are the two major effects of the Gospel?

5. Read Romans 10:17. Where does faith come from?

Discover Meaning

1. On what does the Law focus? On what does the Gospel focus?

2. How does Romans 3:20 keep us clear about the Law's purpose?

3. In 1 Peter 3:15, we are told that Christians are to give an answer for their hope to whomever may ask, with "gentleness and respect." How do we understand these two qualities?

4. John 6:37, 39, 44, and 65 describe how a person comes to Christ. What do they say?

5. How do the categories of *vertical* and *horizontal* help us understand that the Christian is someone who both has peace and does not have peace? that the Christian has both joy and sadness?

EXPLORE IMPLICATIONS

1. Give the two completely different purposes of the Law and Gospel. Why is mixing or confusing their message so detrimental?

2. If one believes in *legalism*, then what are the two problems ("d" words) that often follow? If one believes in *libertinism*, then what problem often follows (another "d" word)?

3. To effectively share the Gospel, the Christian should do so in humility. How does the Christian arrive at humility, and what does it look like?

4. What if a person says, "There is only one thing you have to do to receive the Gospel: you must believe"? How might this confuse the Gospel and return to the Law? How then do we explain the place of faith in the equation of personal conversion?

5. Read Romans 8:31. How does constant confession and absolution reinforce this truth in the face of so much that stands against us?

CHAPTER 12

THE LUTHERAN LENS— CONVERGENCE, 20/20 VISION

In chapter 1, when describing the outside cultural forces that confront Christians, we cited 2 Corinthians 1:8, which reveals that sometimes even believers can feel despair. That's a strong word, but God's Word is realistic and doesn't pull punches. Thank God. The Word of God, therefore, puts us in the position to know what can happen. We are not left to idealism. God's Word is realistic so that we know to take His offer to save us seriously. However, 2 Corinthians 1:8 is not the last word on the topic of despair.

TWO DESPAIRS

In the same Book of 2 Corinthians, St. Paul also wrote this: "We are afflicted in every way, but not crushed; perplexed, but not driven to despair" (2 Corinthians 4:8). Both references use the same core word for *despair*. Well, which is it? Do Christians despair or don't they? The answer is yes, and let us not worry about seeming contradictions. If anything, as we have been looking at the various lenses, we know that these are not contradictions but paradoxes. The lenses of faith are two sides of the same coin. These sides are not contradictory but complementary. Scripture is not therefore putting before us "either-or" propositions, but "both-and" propositions.

How might we take the situation with the biblical word *despair*? Interestingly, the right answer has everything to do with this book's consideration: faith that sees through what the culture and world throw at us. When do Christians despair? They despair when their eyes of faith are taken off Christ. When do Christians not despair, even when confronted by afflictions and perplexities? They do not despair as their eyes of faith are kept on Jesus.

In Exodus 14, the Holy Scriptures record the miracle of the Israelites crossing the Red Sea. Let's try to imagine for a second what it was like to have been there. The people were already skeptical about their overall position in life: "Is it because there are no graves in Egypt that you have taken us away to die in the wilderness?" (Exodus 14:11). They gathered at the edge of the Red Sea and calculated two facts: "On the one hand, we may drown; and on the other hand, we may be slaughtered by Pharaoh and his chariots." In this way, they used their fleshly eyes, and what they saw was reason to despair. Do Christians ever do this? Unfortunately, it happens all the time. Christians can be just like St. Peter, who got off to an amazing start, walking on water while looking at the Lord (Matthew 14:29). This is what Christians do when they keep their eyes of faith on Jesus. They walk through life without despair, confident in the Lord's provision and care, enabled to go forward regardless of the storms and in spite of the waves.

FAITH LENSES: KNOWING THE BIBLICAL DUALITIES

This has been our reason for writing this book: learning to see through the culture by faith. Faith is equipped when we are aware of its various lenses—lenses that help us see with greater understanding, so that we are less susceptible to the discouragements of the world, the devil, and our own sin. The first five chapters covered six components of the Christian life: three that try to get us down, and three others that give us hope. Once again, these are the basic positional or foundational dualities or lenses:

One sees world.	The other sees Christian.
One sees devil.	The other sees disciple.
One sees sin.	The other sees priest.

As mentioned before, consider how the right-hand column will not permit the weaknesses on the left to take over to cause permanent blurriness in life:

The world removes God.	The Word gives Christ.
The devil accuses us.	The Word sustains faith.
Sin says live for self.	The Word says live for others.

That is, the right-hand column gives fortification against the unholy trinity of the left-hand column. As much as the world, the devil, and our sin try to overcome our faith, they are helpless to do so in the face of the Christian's true identity: Christian, disciple, and priest. To be these—what every true Christian is—is to be in Christ, to be equipped by His Word, and to live out the very mission of God. With such clarity of identity in life, it is no wonder that the world is overcome by faith (1 John 5:4), that the devil must flee the one who resists him (James 4:7), and that our sin has been absorbed for us and deflected from us by the blood of Jesus (1 John 2:2).

SIX MORE LENSES THAT HELP
US SEE THROUGH THE CULTURE

The evil one, however, looks for other ways to bring us down, and this was the reason we launched into the six chapters on the lenses of faith. To review, these are the six questions we have sought to answer in a culture that tries desperately to confuse the matter:

What is real?

What am I?

To whom am I speaking?

Where are we?

When are we?

What do I say?

How does the culture in the world try to deceive us in each of these categories? Said in a different way, how does the culture try to discourage faith in relation to these six categories? Notice the last word after each point listed below. This is how we must consider these deceptions against faith. These are the six reasons to strengthen faith that sees through the culture, because the culture says:

"Regarding what is real, only what you physically detect is real." *Lie!*

"Regarding what we are, to know conflict means you're ineffective." *Lie!*

"Regarding to whom you speak, *no* to inclusivity with exclusivity." *Lie!*

"Regarding where you are, you can't live out faith in the state." *Lie!*

"Regarding when you are, God's kingdom is only future, and the devil now reigns." *Lie!*

"Regarding what to say, live out legalism or libertinism, so no Gospel." *Lie!*

THE CULTURE TRIES TO TRAP THE CHRISTIAN

Too often, however, even Christians go along with the lies. It is easy to fall into the first trap. Our propensity is to grant the conventional saying "Seeing is believing." This idea, however, is ludicrous when it is bound only to physical perception. As we discussed, it isn't even logically tenable, much less theologically accurate. We must instead hold to the theology of the cross over and above the theology of glory. We must learn to recognize when God is hidden and yet still very much working in our lives.

Regarding the second trap, too many Christians think that their conflict means defeat; or they take on the false idea of turning their conflict into their idol, believing that they are conducting a kind of glorified penance—that their suffering earns God's help and merit. Wrong! Instead, while the Lord permits our conflict/struggle/battle, which is perfectly normal, we know that it is also purposeful. It is necessary for pulling us away from our insistence for self-salvation. When we see our helpless state, then we are led to call on the name of the Lord. Finally, this leads us to God's solution, which is always Jesus, and then in Him, we are led to life in the Spirit. We begin to see that in being crucified with Christ (something Holy Baptism guarantees), His victory has become our victory, so that defeatism in sin's conflict is an illusion, while the reality is Christ.

The third trap insists that inclusivism cannot be connected to exclusivism. In this way, the world dictates its preferred religion: universalism, which has relativism as its mechanism. In this way, religion is only subjective, and it assumes that faith has no grounding in what is factual, real, or objective. In this case, individuals simply decide to believe in whatever seems right to them. If it is true that faith has no objective grounding (and it isn't), then God is often said to love everyone, but with the caveat "regardless of what they believe." Instead, faith sees that inclusivism and exclusivism are not at all antithetical. Instead, the Gospel demonstrates its power by virtue of an exclusive Savior who guarantees precisely that all have been saved and forgiven. In this section's examples from science, relationships, cultural artifacts, and the Scriptures themselves, we saw why inclusive and exclusive go hand in hand.

The fourth trap insists in the famous cultural motto "separation of church and state." Our culture loves this one, and in some ways, this one might be where Christians are most often tricked. After all, the related theological concepts of the kingdom of power and the kingdom of grace are related to the cultural construct "church and state." The biblical kingdoms are in fact separate, distinct, and serve different purposes. Because of this, Christians might easily go along with the cultural position: "Therefore, keep these far apart." Furthermore, there are *some* ways in which Christians *should* avoid confusion and mixture. This, however, does not mean that these do not interact. Instead, Christians have at least three things at their disposal in the name of faith in the public square: speak the Gospel as St. Paul did in Athens, speak natural law that resonates with good reason, and live out holy vocation (while always being ready to share Law and Gospel one-on-one).

The fifth trap is about time, and it takes the concept of God's reign through His kingdom to be something far away in the future, "because after all," it is reasoned, "just look at the evidence of the devil being in control! Look at all our problems! This world is a mess and God is nowhere to be seen!" Under these assumptions, God's kingdom is not yet here, and instead, evil reigns. These, however, are bald-faced lies. Through the lens of faith, we see that Christ has already bound Satan, who can no longer resist the power of Christ's Word and Sacraments to grant faith to sinners. Satan cannot hold back the power of the Gospel! Jesus has all authority; the devil has none. In the meantime, God permits the problems in the world so that we would never forget that Jesus said that His kingdom is not of this world. This does not mean that Christians despise the creation. Much to the contrary, when Christians know that God's kingdom is among them, they are all the more effective to live as salt and light in the world.

The last trap interferes with what Christians say. God's Law is a great resource for helping people, so the culture and the devil have gone to great strides to confuse what law is. From a worldly perspective, law is used either for self-justification by striving to keep it or it is completely ignored because it is viewed as superfluous and irrelevant. In the first case, the law is used to boost human pride so that one person can look down on another. In the other case, the law is removed so that sin runs amok, and in this way the human conscience begins to die as hearts and minds are hardened by sin going unchecked. In both cases, the Gospel is avoided, because the proper use of God's Law is never known. Christians see past this. Christians therefore want to use His Law properly so that sin is recognized and confessed. Then the Gospel may be shared.

THE LENS OF FAITH SEES THROUGH THE CULTURE

How do these six lenses converge? How do they work together? By the grace of God, they are already packaged together. They are already part of the faith once handed down to us. The question is when and how to employ them. It depends on the situation. It depends on what the Lord puts in front of His Christian-disciple-priest. Let us consider some examples, one example for each of the six lenses.

1. Lens 1: *What is real?* You know of a person who is deeply discouraged and expressing the loss of hope. This gives the impression of pessimism toward God. Reason says, "They don't want to hear anything of the faith." Conventional wisdom says, "Wait for a better time." The lens of faith, however, reminds you that things are often just the opposite of what they appear. It may be that this moment in time is the perfect time to speak to a person about faith. They are crying out. Who will step forward? Who will be mindful that the Lord still says in His Word, "Go and learn what this means: 'I desire mercy, and not sacrifice.' For I came not to call the righteous, but sinners" (Matthew 9:13)? It is the Lord who says, "Weep with those who weep" (Romans 12:15). Coming alongside someone who is suffering—especially when the rest of the world is avoiding them like the plague—is exactly the kind of thing that the theology of the cross motivates. God is hidden in the appearance of weakness and helplessness. This may be the time of greatest hope.

2. Lens 2: *What am I?* Many Christians have been in the place where they are so cognizant of their struggle with sin that they feel ashamed and defeated. In such a case, it is easy to think, "How on earth can I be of any help to another person when I am such a mess?" Such a thought is complemented by the idea "I can't say anything about *that* because I am just as bad." These are indications that the Christian is wallowing in their sin. It is true: Christians are sinners, and they can relate to St. Paul: "I do the very thing I hate" (Romans 7:15). But the great problem here is the next seemingly logical thought: "I must therefore wait until I get my act together." In other words, Christians will do nothing to

witness, because they've convinced themselves that they must wait to be qualified to speak. The problem here is that they will be waiting for a very long time. This is deception, because only one side has been considered. Christians also have been baptized into Christ. Their conflict is not only normal but necessary. It is a struggle God uses to lead Christians not to wallow but to walk by faith and not by sight. Christians are led to their other life secured by Christ: "I have been crucified with Christ. . . . The life I now live . . . I live by faith" (Galatians 2:20). All that would otherwise hold back a Christian's new life was dealt with on Calvary's cross. In the eyes of God, it is gone. It is now time to start living! With this faith, Christians stop waiting. Faith sees what is unseen. Their new life may even be invisible to themselves, but in Christ it is there. No more waiting.

3. Lens 3: *To whom am I speaking?* Christians may encounter certain individuals and frankly be tempted to believe that some are outside the pale of God's unconditional grace. Some people might seem so inclined toward evil that Christians may question whether they should even reach out to them. Jesus did say, after all, that Christians should not "throw [their] pearls before pigs, lest they trample them underfoot and turn to attack [them]" (Matthew 7:6). In this case, God's Word may be so crassly rejected that the Christian must walk away on a given day. This, however, should never change the conviction that abides through the lens of faith. Christians should never give up hope on anyone, no matter how far gone they may seem. The lens of faith in this case is led by the Gospel's 100 percent inclusion of all people. Amazingly, even the one

who threatens to trample the Gospel underfoot is still forgiven by God in Christ. Universal grace teaches us that this must be true. As for that crass rejecter, Christians will pray for him and hope for another day to come for the Gospel to be shared. They are still loved by God. At the same time, Christians will not permit the culture to compromise the Gospel's exclusivity. There is tremendous pressure today to go along with what goes beyond *universal grace* through the false teaching of *universalism*. Universal grace says that Christ died for all and forgives all. Universalism says, "Believe in whatever you want; it doesn't matter." The tempting force here is to believe that such a position is loving, but the exact opposite is true. This position rejects the only Savior. This means the lens of faith drives Christians to maintain that the Gospel is both inclusive and exclusive. Luther helps us to understand that Christ is for all, but it was only Christ sent to save:

> When the merciful Father saw that we were being oppressed through the Law, that we were being held under a curse, and that we could not be liberated from it by anything, He sent His Son into the world, heaped all the sins of all men upon Him, and said to Him: "Be Peter the denier; Paul the persecutor, blasphemer, and assaulter; David the adulterer; the sinner who ate the apple in Paradise; the thief on the cross. In short, be the person of all men, the one who has committed the sins of all men. And see to it that You pay and make satisfaction for them."[63]

---

63   AE 26:280.

4. Lens 4: *Where are we?* Christians today are inundated with the idea of church and state. Unfortunately, the popular conception has some built-in problems. The most drastic problem, though, is the idea of the separation between church and state. This is a serious challenge for Christians, because insofar as "church and state" corresponds to the two kingdoms (the kingdom of power and the kingdom of grace), there are indeed important distinctions. Furthermore, the two kingdoms should not be mingled. All of this tempts us to accept culture's idea of total separation between the two realms. What the culture means, however, is that faith should not be expressed in the public square. Faith must be kept private. Christians should keep faith to themselves. This is a terrible idea and is completely contrary to God's Word. First, Christians are to defend the faith wherever they go. Not only are Christians ready to keep 1 Peter 3:15 to share their specific faith in the Gospel "to anyone who asks you for a reason for the hope that is in you," but Christians may also be equipped in natural law to meet the challenges within the culture, especially in defending marriage, life, and family. What is more, Christians are called to live faithfully in holy vocation, and in this way their very lives are as salt to the earth and light to the world (Matthew 5:13–14). Christians are living testimonies that God is in the culture, even when the culture tries to remove Him.

5. Lens 5: *When are we?* "Now and not yet" will not permit the culture to dictate to us. The world says that God's kingdom is not present. Even many Christians insist that it must all be future. In addition, both the culture and many Christians would have us believe

that the devil is in complete control. This view is terribly pessimistic, but even worse, it is contrary to God's Word. Christians must counter the culture and testify that the kingdom of God is here already. Christians should witness to the fact that the devil is bound. The victorious King of kings and Lord of lords, Jesus Christ, comes to Christians constantly through His Word and Sacraments. This brings the future into the present— the "not yet" into the "now" even though we do not yet see the full glory of what is still to come. These truths instill the Christian with immense confidence. If Christ is in fact reigning now (and He is), and if the devil is already bound (and he is), then St. Paul was and is right: "If God is for us, who can be against us?" (Romans 8:31). The constant reception of the Sacrament guarantees this reality.

6. Lens 6: *What do we say?* The culture clings to its popular value: "Do not judge." In the eyes of the culture, this is not unlike an eleventh commandment. The culture goes beyond what Jesus taught in Matthew 7:1. His teaching not to judge does not mean to avoid discerning between good and evil but to avoid a condemning spirit, or judging for the sake of putting oneself above someone else. It is to behave hypocritically as if one were better than others; as if one were without sin. The culture, however, uses the popular idea to completely misuse the concept of law. In culture's view, the law is either used to justify oneself

(legalism) or it is avoided all together (libertinism). In either case, the proper use of God's Law is lost, and in this way people never come to see the problem of their sin. When this happens, the need for the Gospel is never known either. Salvation is cut off. Christians should never accept the culture's view of God's Law. This means Christians strive to use the Law as it was intended by God to be used: for people to become conscious of sin (Romans 3:20). Then and only then do Christians share the Gospel. Along the way, Christians remember that they are in the same boat as their fellow sinners, and they need the Gospel just as much as anyone.

Remember the phoropter in chapter 6? It reminds us that sometimes two sides need to be brought into alignment. The good doctor uses the phoropter that leads to a prescription for two lenses to work together for clarity of vision. We need the lenses to work together. The same is true of the Christian faith. It is full of *lenses*, or dualities, of the sacred revelation of God's Word. When we get the dualities right, we see with clarity of vision. Then we see through the culture—and anything else—with the lens of faith. We must, however, be in the right position for any of this to occur. The child of God must be *in Christ* and kept in His saving work. The child of God must be a *disciple* who remains steadfast in the Word, the one thing necessary (Luke 10:42). Finally, the child of God must be a *priest* to live out his or her purpose as one who stands between God and others who need to know the Savior.

When this foundation is secure, then Christians can be excited about being continually equipped. They will be able to see more and more to the glory of God and in service to their neighbor. After all, the lens of faith that sees through the culture is already theirs in Jesus Christ. They have His Word. They can see.

THE LUTHERAN LENS—
CONVERGENCE, 20/20 VISION

UNCOVER INFORMATION

1. Do Christians experience *despair* (remember our "both-and" pattern)? Explain.

2. Describe the three pairs of lenses presented in chapters 1–5.

3. What are the six questions that help us learn the six lenses in chapters 6–11?

4. According to Scripture, what is real?

5. According to Scripture, *where* is the Christian?

DISCOVER MEANING

1. Consider Matthew 14:22–33. When did St. Peter despair? When did he *not* despair?

2. Why are the three right-column gifts greater than the three left-column burdens?

3. What are the lies spoken by the culture against each of these six lenses?

4. Regarding *what we are*: how does the fact that we have been crucified impart a sense of freedom and liberation to live the Christian life?

5. Since Jesus has already bound the devil, how does this help the Christian see current conditions even while they seem so dire?

EXPLORE IMPLICATIONS

1. With this *despair duality* also in our lives, how do *we* have Jesus kept before *us*?

2. Note that every right-column gift has the Word. Discuss how the Word remains in our lives in three spheres: (a) individually; (b) family and/or small group; (c) congregationally.

3. When you consider how Christians respond to the cultural traps, what kind of outlook, attitude, and/or disposition should accompany the Christian's response?

4. Review the words of Luther about what Christ became when the Father sent Him. How do these words help Christians when considering those to whom they are speaking about the Gospel?

5. How do legalism and libertinism threaten to cut off the proper reception of the saving Gospel? If it appears someone is holding to one of these, how should the Christian respond?

BIBLIOGRAPHY

Chemnitz, Martin. *Loci Theologici*. Vol. II. Translated by J. A. O. Preus. St. Louis: Concordia Publishing House, 1989.

Concordia: The Lutheran Confessions. Second Edition. St. Louis: Concordia Publishing House, 2006.

Das, Andrew A. *Galatians,* Concordia Commentary. St. Louis: Concordia Publishing House, 2014.

Espinosa, Alfonso Odilon. "The Apocalyptic Anxiety of American Evangelicalism As Seen Through Left Behind and Tim LaHaye's Programme for the Preservation of Evangelical Identity." PhD dissertation, University of Birmingham (England), 2009.

Franzmann, Martin H. *Romans: A Commentary*. St. Louis: Concordia Publishing House, 1968.

Ludwig, Garth D. *Order Restored: A Biblical Interpretation of Health Medicine and Healing*. St. Louis: Concordia Publishing House, 1999.

Luther, Martin. *Career of the Reformer: I*. Vol. 31 of Luther's Works. Edited by Harold J. Grimm. Philadelphia: Fortress Press, 1957.

———. *Career of the Reformer: III*. Vol. 33 of Luther's Works. Edited by Philip S. Watson. Philadelphia: Fortress Press, 1972.

———. *Christian in Society: III*. Vol. 46 of Luther's Works. Edited by Robert C. Schultz. Philadelphia: Fortress Press, 1967.

———. *Lectures on Galatians 1535: Chapters 1–4*. Vol. 26 of Luther's Works. Edited by Jaroslav Pelikan. St. Louis: Concordia Publishing House, 1963.

———. *The Sermon on the Mount and the Magnificat*. Vol. 21 of Luther's Works. Edited by Jaroslav Pelikan. St. Louis: Concordia Publishing House, 1956.

———. *Word and Sacrament: I*. Vol. 35 of Luther's Works. Edited Theodore Bachmann. Philadelphia: Fortress Press, 1960.

———. *Word and Sacrament: III*. Vol. 37 of Luther's Works, Edited by Robert H. Fischer. Philadelphia: Fortress Press, 1961.

Lutheran Service Book. St. Louis: Concordia Publishing House, 2006.

Middendorf, Michael P. *Romans 1–8*, Concordia Commentary. St. Louis: Concordia Publishing House, 2013.

Peters, Albrecht. *Commentary on Luther's Catechisms: Baptism and Lord's Supper*. St. Louis: Concordia Publishing House, 2012.

Pieper, Francis. *Christian Dogmatics*. Vol. I. St. Louis: Concordia Publishing House, 1950.

Walther, C. F. W. *Law and Gospel: How to Read and Apply the Bible*. Edited by Charles P. Schaum. Translated by Christian C. Tiews. St. Louis: Concordia Publishing House, 2010.

TOPICAL INDEX

A

Abortion 164, 176–77
Accuser 38
American Christianity 113
Amos 27
Anguish replaced by joy 44
Antinomianism 217
Anxiety 122, 156, 191, 193
Apologetics 30, 66
Assyrian/Assyria 27, 28, 94
Atheism 29, 162
Atonement 52, 53

B

Baptism 18, 30, 39, 48, 49, 50, 98, 122
Basic needs 82
Batman 76
Body and spirit 92
Born again/from above 39, 51, 197

C

Christian 44, 48, 49, 51, 99, 111, 136, 150
Christian nation 150, 168
Christ's circumcision 95
Christ's two natures 19, 95
Church and state 161, 169, 246, 251
Church 160, 161, 162, 181
Church attendance 183
Communion 18, 201–03
Complementarity, inclusive and exclusive 128, 139, 140, 141, 142, 145

Conflict within Christian 98, 99, 101, 102, 111, 112, 113, 118, 122, 199
Contentment 34, 35
Conscience 219
Conversion 78
Conviction, Contrition, Confession, Consolation and Consecration 152
Creation 22, 46, 70
Credentials of Christian faith 144
Cross 101
Culture 19, 20, 22, 23, 24, 27, 81, 165
Culture lenses 247
Culture traps 245
Cyrus 167

D

Darby 192
Debased mind 218
Delusion 113, 214
Demonic 25, 194
Despair 26, 102, 113, 216, 241
Devil 25, 194, 197
Disciple 60, 63, 68, 69, 71
Dispensationalism 192
Divine Service 181
Dual citizenship 160
Dualities 90, 242

E

Election 219, 220
Einstein 91, 199
Elijah 34
Eternal life 78
Evil in culture 27
Exclusivity 137
Exorcism 25
Expiation 55

F

Faith 16, 18, 29–31, 40, 45, 46, 48, 70, 94, 96, 98, 107, 121, 223
Fear 38
Fighting God 38
First Gospel 194–95
Flesh 118–19
Four forces 116
Future 190

G

God hiding 94
Gospel 44, 45, 58, 128, 136, 137, 210, 222, 223, 226, 228
Great Commission 75
Great Depression 28, 35
Great reversal 49, 107, 108
Greatest generation 28

H

Heavenly 92–93
Heidelberg Disputation 99, 102
Hiddenness of God 96
Historical fact of the Gospel 79
Holy Cross 199
Holy Spirit 45, 51, 63, 111, 117, 119, 122, 124–25, 152, 197, 198, 199, 211–12
Horizontal and vertical 230
Humility 100, 221, 222
Humiliation, Christ's 95
Hymns 71, 95

I

Idolatry 28
Image of God 37

Immortality 27–28
In Christ 49
Inclusivity 129, 138
Individual Confession and Absolution 233, 235
Inheritance 51
Invisible Church 181
Israel 27
Ivory houses 28

J

Jesus, complementarity inclusivity and exclusivity 145
Joachim of Fiore 192
Justification 58

K

Kingdom of God 160, 161, 165, 194

L

Labels 129, 150
Law and Gospel 66, 209, 238
Legalism 214, 216
Levels of Christians/ Stages of Christian development 113–14
Libertine 217
Love 81, 129–31, 133, 136, 179, 180, 221
Luther 29, 50, 63, 99–103, 114, 121, 161, 170, 177–79, 180, 182, 199, 213, 235, 250
Lutheran 20

M

Marriage 17, 102, 104–06, 141, 163–64, 174–75
Means of Grace 40, 98
Messianic expectations 94
Mexican restaurant/ food 47, 142
Michelangelo's *The Last Judgment* 155
Militaristic proclamation 44
Millennial kingdom 192–97
Moralist 150

N

Naaman 97
Natural law 163
New status 48, 50
Normal Christian life 122
Now and not yet 190, 205

P

Paradise 78
Paradoxes 90
Passively crucified 120
Peace 228, 230
Phoropter 89, 253
Physical versus spiritual maladies 25
Politics 161, 167
Prayer 106
Presumption of righteousness 213
Presuppositions 65
Prevenient grace 16
Priest 75, 79
Priority of present 189–90
Propitiation 53
Public square 162

R

Reconciliation 57
Redemption 56
Religious liberty 162, 174
Resurrection of the body 78
Revelation, Book of 193, 195–97
Reversal 49, 107, 108

Rome 29

S

Sacraments 16, 18, 96
Secularism 29
Self-absorption 191
Self-centeredness 81
Separation of church and state 29
Sermon on the Mount 24
Shame 38, 49
Sin/Sinful 37, 39
Solomon 23, 27, 28, 167
Spiritual organ 16, 45
Spiritual realm 92
State 160
Substitutional 45, 51

T

Theist 150
Theocratic nation 28
Theology of glory 101
Theology of the cross 101
Thorn in the flesh 25
Tolerance 25
Tree of knowledge of good and evil 37
Trifecta identity of Christians 81
Triumphalism 113
Two kinds of works 179
Two kingdoms 160

U

Unholy trinity 39
Universal grace 131, 132

V

Vicarious 51
Visible and invisible 91
Vocation 170, 178

W

Walther 100, 101, 210, 215, 220, 222–23,

225–26, 230–31,
237–38
Wholeness 206
Widow of Zarephath
34
Will, Human 223–27
Word 63, 70–72
World 19, 29, 36
World War II 28, 39
Worldliness 24
Worship 71, 184

SCRIPTURE INDEX

Genesis
1:3: p. 63
1:31: p. 22
2:17: p. 37
3: pp. 37, 49, 57
3:5: p. 192
3:7–8: p. 38
3:15: pp. 195, 207
11:4: p. 191
38: p. 146

Exodus
14: p. 242
14:11: p. 242
20:3: p. 215

Leviticus
17:11: pp. 52, 61

Deuteronomy
6:4–9: pp. 69, 74
21:23: p. 96

Joshua
2 and 6: 146

1 Samuel
18:1: p. 141

2 Samuel
11: p. 146

1 Kings
6:20: p. 197
17: p. 35
22:39: p. 28

2 Kings
5: p. 110
5:1: p. 97
5:5: p. 97
5:10–14: p. 98

Ezra
1:1: p. 167

Job
19:25–27: p. 204

Psalm
19:1: p. 22
22: p. 229
30:5: p. 111
32:1–2: pp. 12, 59
42:1: p. 235
51:5: p. 37
90:12: pp. 190, 208
118:24: pp. 189, 207
119:105: pp. 69, 73

Proverbs
14:12: p. 100

Ecclesiastes
9:7: p. 23

Isaiah
9:6: p. 229
43:25: pp. 55, 62, 236
44:28: pp. 168, 188
55:8–9: p. 100

Ezekiel
36:25–27: p. 225

Amos
3:15: p. 28

Matthew
1: p. 146
1:3, 5, 6: p. 146
4:11: p. 93
5:4: p. 231
5:6: p. 232
5:10: p. 24
5:10–12: p. 229
5:13–14: pp. 165, 188, 251
5:16: p. 81
5:22, 28: p. 214
6:34: pp. 190, 193, 208

7:1: p. 252
7:6: p. 249
9: p. 147
9:10–11: p. 147
9:12–13: p. 147
9:13: p. 248
10:28: p. 205
10:34: p. 229
11:28. pp. 122, 137, 177
13:24–30: p. 182
14:22–33: p. 254
14:29: p. 242
15:8: p. 183
16:15: p. 145
16:17: p. 118
16:18: p. 197
16:24: pp. 102, 200
18:20: p. 203
18:22: p. 236
19:16–22: p. 214
19:26: p. 202
20:28: p. 81
22:21: p. 166
23:37: p. 220
24:12: p. 81
25: pp. 155, 156
25:40: p. 189
26:26, 28: p. 202
26:28: p. 197
26:53: p. 95
27:39–43: p. 96
28: p. 75
28:18: p. 196
28:19: p. 87
28:19–20: p. 87

Mark
10:16: p. 177
10:45: p. 56
14:22, 24: p. 202

Luke
2:14: p. 229
7: pp. 147, 226
8: p. 148
10:41–42: pp. 70, 74
10:42: pp. 223, 253

11:20: p. 194
12:32: p. 185
15: pp. 148, 218
15:12–19: p. 218
17:21: p. 162
18:9–14: p. 108
22:19–20: p. 202
23:43: pp. 78, 87
24:47: p. 136

John

1:1, 14: p. 50
1:12–13: p. 121
1:29: pp. 55, 137
3:3–7: pp. 39, 43, 51
3:5: p. 197
3:16: pp. 87, 88, 130, 136, 158
3:16–17: p. 79
4: p. 148
4:14: p. 139
5:24: pp. 39, 78, 87, 204
6:29: p. 48
6:37: pp. 224, 239
6:39: pp. 224, 239
6:40: p. 137
6:44: pp. 224, 239
6:51: p. 137
6:60: p. 199
6:65: pp. 224, 239
6:66: p. 199
8:31–32: pp. 69, 74
8:34: p. 56
8:44: p. 26
10:10: p. 53
10:28: p. 232
11:35: p. 95
11:43–44: pp. 63, 73
13:34: p. 54
14:6: p. 138, 158
15:13: p. 157
15:16: pp. 48, 225
15:20: p. 229
16:21: p. 44
18:33: p. 187
18:36: pp. 165, 168, 169, 187, 196
19:10: p. 166
19:11: p. 166

19:30: pp. 54, 131, 195
20: p. 148

Acts

2:36: p. 211
2:37: p. 211
11:26: p. 48
17:23: p. 163
17:28: pp. 70, 191

Romans

1:16: pp. 45, 79
1:28–32: p. 218
2:14–15: p. 164
2:15: p. 217
3:20: pp. 154, 211, 239, 253
3:22: p. 137
3:23: pp. 213, 219
4:5: p. 59
4:7–8: p. 59
5: pp. 30, 158
5:6, 8, 10: pp. 130, 158
5:10–11: p. 57
6:3–4: p. 122
6:23: p. 215
7: pp. 115, 119
7:12: p. 116
7:15: p. 248
7:18–23: p. 115
7:19: p. 213
7:22–23: p. 116
7:24–25: p. 116
8: pp. 115, 117, 127
8:3–4: p. 117
8:28: pp. 93, 106, 110, 232
8:31: pp. 106, 204. 232, 240, 252
8:33–34, 39: p. 59
10:12: p. 137
10:17: pp. 16, 68, 73, 227, 239
11:32: p. 137
12:2: p. 114
12:9: p. 54
12:15: pp. 185, 248
13:1–6: p. 167
14:17: p. 196

1 Corinthians

7:5: p. 182
9:22: p. 237
11:24–25: p. 202
11:29: p. 202
12: p. 181
15:42–43: p. 204

2 Corinthians

1:8: pp. 27, 241
4:8: p. 241
4:10–11: p. 12
4:17–18: p. 99
5:7: pp. 19, 93, 109
5:17: p. 198
5:21: p. 54
12:7: pp. 25, 118
12:7–12: p. 104
12:9: p. 12

Galatians

2:17: p. 121
2:19–20: pp. 120
2:20: p. 249
3:13: p. 57
3:27–28: p. 121
4: p. 12
4:4: p. 95
5: pp. 115, 118, 119, 120, 126
5:16: p. 118
5:17: p. 118
5:16–18: p. 117
5:22–23: pp. 69, 74, 198
5:24: pp. 119, 120
6:14: p. 120

Ephesians

2:1: p. 63
2:10: pp. 81, 121
4: p. 14
5:15–16: p. 190
5:27: p. 197
6: p. 93
6:12: pp. 92, 109
6:16: p. 26

Philippians

1:20: p. 190
1:21–24: p. 231
1:22: pp. 189, 207
3:7–8: p. 12
3:14: pp. 190, 207
4:4–7: p. 205
4:8–9: p. 70

Colossians

1:13–14: p. 182
3:17: p. 172

1 Timothy

1:15: p. 221
2:4: pp. 75, 88
2:8: p. 235
4:1–3: p. 218
6:6–7: pp. 35, 42

2 Timothy

1:9: p. 55
2:26: p. 56

Hebrews

3:7–8: p. 212
3:15: pp. 212, 232
4:7: p. 212
8:12: p. 236
10:25: p. 181
11:1: p. 12
11:16: p. 34
13:5: p. 232

James

2:10: p. 213
4:7: pp. 198, 243

1 Peter

2:9: pp. 80, 87
2:11: pp. 37, 42
3:2: p. 83
3:15: pp. 80, 84, 87, 88,
    165, 221, 239, 251
3:21: p. 39
4:12: p. 199
5:8: pp. 25, 26

2 Peter

3:9: p. 137

1 John

1:7: p. 137
2:2: pp. 54, 79, 88, 137,
    243
2:15–16: p. 36
2:15–17: p. 32
3:4: p. 209
3:8: p. 119
4:8, 16: pp. 130, 158
4:18: pp. 124, 228
4:19: p. 81
5:4: pp. 112, 243

Revelation

3: p. 224
3:20: p. 224
12:10: p. 38
14:13: p. 102
20:2: pp. 195, 196
20:3: p. 197
21:16: p. 197